GALA

DIABETES, HIGH BLOOD PRESSURE, WITHOUT ANY FEAR

by

Dr. Dhiren Gala
B.Sc., D.H.M.S., D.O., D.Ac.,
C.G.O., C.C.H., A.R.S.H.

With

Dr. D. R. Gala
N.D., D.N.O., D.C.O.

Dr. Sanjay Gala
M.B.(BOM.), M.S. (FNT)

NAVNEET PUBLICATIONS (INDIA) LIMITED

Navneet House, Gurukul Road, Memnagar, Ahmadabad – 380 052. Phone : 2743 6300 / 2743 9300	**Navneet Bhavan,** B. S. Road, Dadar, Mumbai – 400 028. Phone : 5662 6565

DHANLAL BROTHERS DISTRIBUTORS
70, Princess Street, Mumbai – 400 002.
Phone : 2201 7027

e-mail : dhanlal@vsnl.net

Visit us at : www.navneet.com & connectschool.com

e-mail : npil@navneet.com

Price : Rs. 50.00

Dr. D. R. Gala

1st floor, Abbas Building 'A',
Near Tilak Market, Jalbhai Lane,
Harkishandas Hospital Road,
Grant Road (East), Mumbai – 400 004.
Phone : 2386 7275

Time : 4.00 to 7.00 pm

[19 – 5 – 2003 (12) : 5]

PREFACE

The incidence of Diabetes Mellitus and High Blood Pressure is rising at an alarming pace in our country. Diabetes and High Blood Pressure are dreadful and life-time diseases. Unless adequately controlled, they throw all the systems and organs of the body into disarray and give rise to terrible complications.

Extraordinary perseverance and intelligent planning are required to combat these two diseases and the patient has to be his own commander. To fight this battle successfully, it is necessary that the patient possesses the knowledge of all the aspects of these diseases. However, it is not easy for common people to acquire all the knowledge about these diseases. Besides, even a doctor cannot fully educate his patients about these diseases because of several limitations, especially that of time. That is precisely the reason to bring out this book. If a reader afflicted by any of these two diseases assiduously follows the suggestions given in this book, we are sure he shall be able to lead an active and productive life.

Today, many fallacious ideas and myths about these two diseases prevail in the minds of lay people. Such myths have been exploded in this book.

The guidelines for treatment, given in many a book available in the market, most of which are by foreign authors, cannot be wholly applied to Indian conditions. This book tries to eliminate such flaws.

We are thankful to Dr. Ashok Patel from Ahmadabad and Dr. Amrut Vora from Mumbai for going through the manuscript of this book and offering valuable suggestions.

Constructive suggestions from laymen and experts alike, for the improvement of this book, shall be gratefully acknowledged.

—**Authors**

CONTENTS

PART I : DIABETES MELLITUS

1. INTRODUCTION

Diseases are of two types : (1) Infectious and (2) Constitutional. Infectious diseases are caused by bacteria or viruses coming from without; constitutional diseases are caused by untoward changes occurring within the body.

Until the end of the first decade of this century, infectious diseases predominated. During epidemics, such diseases spread like wild-fires and took a heavy toll of human life. However, with the advent of antibiotics and effective vaccines against polio, smallpox, diphtheria, etc., the incidence of infectious diseases started to wane. On the other hand diseases of civilisation (or urbanisation) like high blood pressure, coronary heart disease and cancer increased steadily.

Diabetes Mellitus is also such a constitutional disease. It is an outcome of leading a sedentary life and eating processed foods. The incidence of diabetes varies directly with the consumption of processed foods like biscuits, bread, cakes, chocolates, pudding, ice-cream, etc.

The number of people afflicted by diabetes is increasing each day. Today, 3 to 12 per cent of the population of the world has either established diabetes or a tendency of contracting it in the near future. At present, about 75,00,000 Indians suffer from diabetes. The total figure is expected to cross the one crore mark by the end of this century. Thus, the problem of diabetes is monstrous in magnitude.

The incidence of diabetes is greater in our cities than in our villages.

The following statistical data clearly brings home this fact :

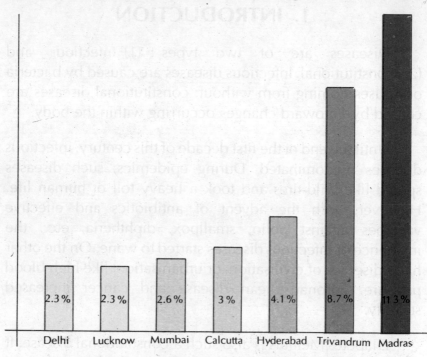

Delhi	Lucknow	Mumbai	Calcutta	Hyderabad	Trivandrum	Madras
2.3 %	2.3 %	2.6 %	3 %	4.1 %	8.7 %	11 3 %

Fig. 1.1 : Incidence of diabetes in chief Indian cities

However, the disease is now making inroads into the Indian villages as well. There, due to the absence of adequate diagnostic or treatment facilities, the situation is very grim.

Though it is true that diabetes is extremely rampant today, it is not a new disease. Well-known Ayurvedic physicians Maharshi Charaka (600 B.C.) and Sushruta (400 B.C.) correctly described almost all the symptoms of this disease. They called the disease Madhu-meha (a shower of honey). Ancient Ayurvedic text 'Sushruta-Samhita' clearly states that diabetes is a familiar disease. Inspite of total absence of the basic knowledge about human anatomy, physiology and biochemistry, Charaka and Sushruta have displayed remarkable understanding of the disease.

A methodical study of human anatomy and physiology began about 200 years back. In 1869 A. D., Paul Langerhans discovered the islet cells responsible for the metabolism of sugar inside the body. These islets were later named, after their discoverer, as islets of Langerhans. In 1889 A. D., Won Mering and Oscar Minkowski succeeded in artificially producing diabetes in a dog, by removing its pancreas gland. This experiment brought great laurels to the two scientists because the relation between diabetes and pancreas was revealed. In 1909 A. D., D'Mayer named the extract of pancreas as insulin. In 1920 A. D., Fredrick Banting and Charles Best managed to isolate pure insulin from the pancreatic extract. They also showed that when insulin is injected into the bodies of diabetic animals the concentration of sugar in their blood rapidly falls. These important findings fetched the two scientists, the coveted Nobel Prize.

Fredrick Banting   Charles Best

Fig. 1.2 : The discoverers of insulin

After the discovery of insulin, people had started believing that diabetes will soon be banished from the earth. This belief has however proved fallacious. The reasons for this have been explained in the chapters to come.

However, it can be said that insulin has robbed diabetes of its fatality. Fifty years ago, the treatment of diabetes was totally unsatisfactory. Diabetes gave rise to more and severe complications. If a child was diagnosed as a diabetic on his birthday, he seldom lived to celebrate his next birthday. On the other hand, with the advance of medical science and advent of a number of antidiabetic drugs, a diabetic can today look forward to leading an almost normal and creative life.

Even then, it has to be conceded that though with present knowledge and treatment, the concentration of glucose in the blood can be maintained within the normal range, or glucose can be prevented from escaping in the urine, the long-term complications of diabetes cannot be fully checked. In other words, drugs have been able to prolong life; but they have not contributed to the enhancement of the quality of life. That is the reason why diabetes should be prevented.

Chapter in a nutshell :

1. Diabetes is a 'disease of civilisation'. It is a constitutional disease and not contagious.
2. A sedentary life and an excessive intake of carbohydrate-containing foods precipitate diabetes.
3. After the discovery of insulin, people started believing that diabetes shall soon be eradicated. This, however, has turned out to be a dream.
4. With vigorous treatment, short-term complications of diabetes can be checked; but its long-term complications can hardly be prevented.
5. Even then, by educating oneself about the various aspects of the disease, a diabetic can lead a long and happy life.

---

2. WHAT IS DIABETES MELLITUS?

Diabetes is a metabolic disorder, arising either due to (1) relative or absolute deficiency of a digestive hormone called insulin of (2) inability or resistance of body-cells to use the available insulin. The disorder completely throws the metabolism of dietary carbohydrates, fats and proteins into disarray.

To gain a clear understanding of the disease it is necessary to procure basic knowledge about the pancreas gland and the fuction of its secretion insulin in the body.

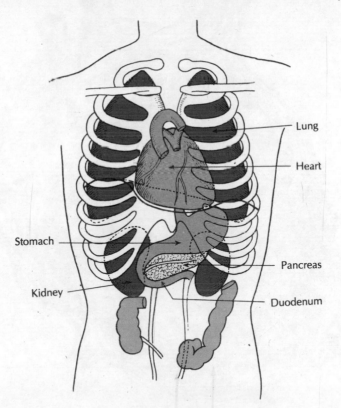

Fig. 2.1 : The pancreas gland

Pancreas is a digestive gland, which lies deep in the upper part of the abdomen, between the lower border of stomach and the upper border of duodenum. On either side, it is flanked by kidneys. The human pancreas weighs about 100 gms and is made up of small units called lobules. Each lobule consists of two groups of cells, the exocrine and the endocrine. Each endocrine group of cells is also called an islet of Langerhans. The beta cells of the islets produce insulin whereas the alpha cells of the islets produce a hormone glucogon, whose action is opposite to that of insulin.

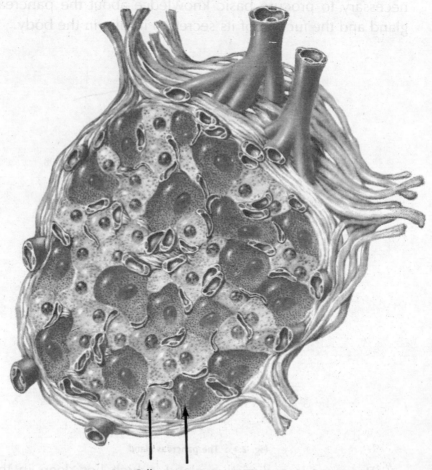

Beta Cells   Alpha Cells

Fig. 2.2 : Islets of Langerhans

The Role of Insulin :

The carbohydrates in our food are digested in the intestines. The end-products of carbohydrate-digestion are various sugars, chiefly glucose. This glucose is absorbed through the mucous membrane of intestines to enter the blood-stream. Thus the concentration of glucose in the blood rises. Insulin makes this glucose available to each and every cell of the body. Each cell in our body is a tiny engine that uses glucose as fuel to generate heat and energy. If glucose-fuel is to gain entrance into the cellular engine, insulin is essential.

Fig. 2.3 : The cellular engine

If the amount of glucose in the blood is greater than the cellular requirements, insulin converts it into glycogen and fat which are stored in the liver (or muscles) and adipose tissue respectively.

Insulin is also concerned with the metabolism of dietary fats and proteins. The end-products of fat-digestion are fatty acids. Insulin converts these fatty acids back into fat and stores it in the adipose tissue. Again, insulin prevents the conversion of stored fat into fatty acids. Insulin is also essential for protein-synthesis in the body. If there is a deficiency of insulin, proteins lost due to wear and tear cannot be replaced.

Besides, insulin also serves certain other functions, the exact nature of which is not yet completely understood.

In short, the most important and obvious function of insulin is to control the concentration of glucose in the blood. After taking food, the concentration of glucose in blood rises. Insulin prevents the glucose concentration to rise above normal or physiological limits.

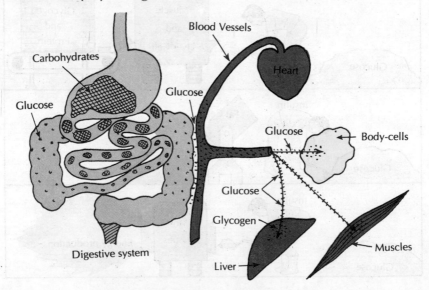

Fig. 2.4 : The distribution of glucose by insulin

If insulin is inadequate or absent, the glucose in blood cannot enter various body-cells or cannot be converted into glycogen. Consequently, blood-glucose level rises.

When the blood passes through the kidneys, the glucose is normally not allowed to escape in the urine. However, when due to lack of insulin, the concentration of glucose increases beyond a particular level, it surpasses the efficiency level of kidneys (called renal threshold) and spills into the urine. That is the reason why the urine of diabetics is sweet.

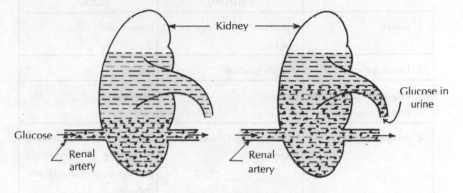

Fig. 2.5 : The spilling of glucose into the urine

Let us again consider cellular nutrition. Normally the nutritional requirements of body-cells are satisfied by glucose. When due to deficiency of insulin or due to resistance of cells to insulin, glucose cannot enter the cells, cellular starvation ensues. To supply nutrition to the starving cells, the body starts disintegrating stored fats and proteins. It is because of the destruction of muscle-protein and fats that a diabetic experiences undue weakness or fatigue and weight-loss respectively.

While defining diabetes, it was said that it is a condition arising due either to (1) deficiency of insulin or (2) inability of body-cells to use available insulin. The first type of diabetes is called Juvenile or insulin dependent diabetes mellitus (IDDM). It afflicts mostly children or young adults and produces acute symptoms. The second type of diabetes is called non-insulin-dependent or maturity onset diabetes mellitus (NIDDM). It mostly afflicts middle-aged persons and produces mild symptoms.* In our country, almost 99 % of all diabetics suffer from the latter variety of diabetes.

Differences between the two types of diabetes have been made clear in the following table :

	Maturity onset diabetes (NIDDM)	Juvenile diabetes (IDDM)
1. Onset	Usually after the age of 35 years	Usually in childhood
2. Development	Usually gradual	Rapid
3. Physical state at the time of onset	Obesity	Leanness
4. Symptoms	Usually absent in the initial stages	Dramatic symptoms comprising of a triad of polydipsia, polyphagia and polyurea
5. Enlargement of liver	Absent	Present
6. Concentration of glucose in blood	Absence of wide fluctuations	Wide fluctuations seen
7. Control of the disease	Less difficult	Very difficult
8. Ketosis	Usually absent	Very common

---

* Though this classification can be applied to most diabetics, exceptional cases are seen. About 15 per cent of adult (maturity onset) diabetics are seen to be insulin-dependent. On the other hand, about 5 per cent of juvenile diabetics have a mild form of the disease. The condition is called 'maturity onset diabetes in the young (MODY)'.

	Maturity onset diabetes (NIDDM)	Juvenile diabetes (IDDM)
9. Amount of insulin in blood	Normal in 38% patients; slightly less than normal in the remaining 62% patients	Negligible or absent
10. Complications of diabetes	Very common	Less common; however, since juvenile diabetics are now living longer and longer, the incidence of complications is gradually rising.
11. Diet-control	Essential	Inevitable
12. Insulin	Neccessary for 20-30% patients	Necessary for all patients
13. Oral drugs	Useful	Usually useless

Chapter in a nutshell :

1. The end-products of carbohydrate-digestion are simple sugars (e. g., glucose). From the intestines, this sugar gets absorbed into the blood-stream. Consequently, the blood-sugar level rises.

2. At this time, the pancreatic secretion insulin enters the blood-stream and strives to bring down the blood-glucose level.

3. If there is a deficiency of insulin or if the available insulin cannot be utilised by the body, the blood-sugar level rises abnormally. This sugar, accumulated in the blood, finally spills over into the urine. This disorder is termed 'diabetes mellitus'.

4. There are two types of diabetes : juvenile or insulin dependent diabetes mellitus (IDDM) and maturity onset or non-insulin-dependent diabetes mellitus (NIDDM).

5. In our country, the incidence of juvenile diabetes is barely 1 – 2 %. The rest of the patients suffer from the second variety of the disease.

6. Juvenile diabetes and maturity onset diabetes differ somewhat in their symptoms and treatment.

3. COMPLICATIONS OF DIABETES

Diabetes has been described, and aptly so, as a disease of complications. The complications of diabetes are more agonising and torturing than the disease itself. Acute complications can arise at any time during the course of the disease, whereas the more dreaded chronic complications slowly unfold themselves years after the onset of diabetes. Many a time, a presenting complication leads to the diagnosis of the disease. Zealous control of diabetes does help in warding off its acute complications; but whether it delays or mitigates the chronic complications or not is a controversial issue. That is the reason why prevention of diabetes assumes special importance.

Acute Complications of Diabetes :

(1) **Diabetic Coma (Unconsciousness) :** Diabetic coma is commonly seen in juvenile (child or young) diabetics but is uncommon in persons suffering from maturity onset diabetes.

Before the discovery of insulin, more than half of juvenile diabetics died of diabetic coma. Today, however, the mortality rate due to this complication has been brought down to 1 – 2 %, thanks to effective treatment with insulin.

This type of unconciousness ensues when the concentration of glucose in the blood rises much above normal, a condition called hyperglycemia. The disintegration of stored fat inside the body is commensurate with the amount of glucose in blood. The end-products of fat-disintegration are ketone bodies, which due to their acidic nature, render the blood acidic. The body tries to get rid of these harmful ketone bodies by producing more and more urine. This, however, results into a reduction in the fluid content of the blood, thereby increasing the concentration of

17

ketone bodies. Thus a vicious circle sets in. This acidified blood untowardly affects the brain to give rise, first to drowsiness and lethargy and then gradually to diabetic coma.

The probable causes for the rise of glucose in blood are :

(1) Undetected or untreated diabetes.

(2) Consumption of carbohydrate-containing refined foods, especially sugar.

(3) Inadequacy or total lack of external (medicinal) insulin.

(4) Development of resistance inside the body to medicinal insulin.

(5) A decrease in the effectiveness of medicinal insulin due to some other infection or disease.

(6) A stressful physical condition like surgery or pregnancy.

It should be borne in mind that a diabetic may become unconcious even when the concentration of glucose in the blood drops much below normal (a condition called hypoglycemia). However, such unconciousness ensues rapidly. On the other hand, unconsciousness due to excessive glucose and ketosis is a slowly developing condition. Hours or days before its advent, a patient experiences symptoms like dryness of mouth, acute thirst, profuse urination, headaches, nausea vomitting, abdominal pain, weakness, laboured breathing, irrelevant answers to questions and drowsiness. Of these symptoms nausea-vomitting, drowsiness and irrelevant answers to asked questions are probably the most common. If the seriousness of the situation is not realised and the patient not treated promptly, he gradually becomes unconscious. However, in some child diabetics, hyper-glycemic coma has been seen to set in very fast, i. e., in 12 to 24 hours.

Diabetic coma is a medical emergency and calls for urgent, expert treatment. The patient should be immediately hospitalised so that he can be given insulin, fluids and salts like potassium through a vein and be constantly monitored.

In fact, hyperglycemic coma should not in the first place be allowed to occur. Its prevention is relatively easy provided –

(1) The patient has adequate knowledge of the disease and its treatment,

(2) The concentration of glucose in blood is not allowed to rise by fastidiously adhering to correct, timely diet and medicines,

(3) The dosage of insulin is maintained (not altered) even if food is not taken in other illnesses,

(4) Even the most initial warning signs and symptoms of hyperglycemia, described above, are immediately heeded to and necessary steps are taken.

A diabetic who experiences one or more of the above symptoms should take complete rest, have a lot of fluids and examine his own urine 3 –4 times a day for presence of sugar and acetone (methods described in chapter 6). If acetone is detected in urine, he should immediately call for his doctor, and should increase the dosage of insulin/oral medicines as per the doctor's advice.

For the reader's ready and 'at a glance' reference the distinguishing features of hyperglycemic coma and hypoglycemic coma have been tabled below :

	Hypoglycemic Coma	Hyperglycemic Coma
1. Onset	Rapid (within minutes)	Gradual (after days)
2. Cause	Excessive medication or physical labour; Inadequate food	Ignorance or carelessness about treatment; some other infection or disease.

3. Symptoms

Thirst	Absent	Present
Hunger	Extreme	Absent
Vomitting	Rare	Very common
Abdominal pain	Absent	Very common
Skin	Moist	Dry
Tremors	Common	Absent
Eyeballs	Normal	Soft
Pulse	Fast (or normal) and strong	Fast and feeble
Breathing	Normal or shallow; odourless	Deep, fast, laboured; with smell of acetone
Appearance of the patient	Pale, weak	Florid, hungry

It is desirable for every diabetic to keep in his pocket an indetification card, which besides mentioning that he is a diabetic, bears his and his doctor's name and address and the type of antidiabetic treatment he is undergoing. This

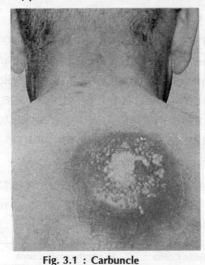

will prevent many mishaps to which a diabetic is liable.

(2) Boils and carbuncles : Recurrent boils and carbuncles may, in fact, be the first indication of diabetes. The factors responsible for this complication are : (a) high glucose-level in the blood vessels of the skin and (b) poor resistance-power against pus-forming micro-organisms.

Fig. 3.1 : Carbuncle

(3) Acute gangrene : Gangrene is defined as the death of a mass of tissue or an organ. Gangrene of a toe or a foot is 50 to 60 times more common in diabetics than in healthy persons. Without adequate care, even a trivial injury to a toe or foot may terminate into gangrene.

Narrowing of the blood-vessels, poor resistance power and untoward changes of the nervous system are said to be responsible for such proneness of diabetics to gangrene. Gangrene usually necessitates amputation of the affected part, to keep the patient alive. Before the advent of insulin, 50% of the diabetics would have died if gangrene supervened. But today, thanks to insulin, antibiotics and medical care, this mortality rate has fallen below 7% and amputations are on the wane.

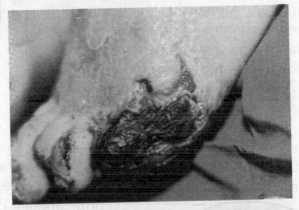

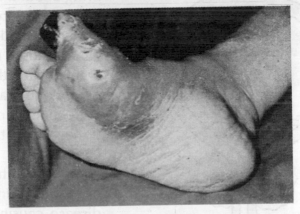

Fig. 3.2 : Acute gangrene

Chronic or late complications of diabetes :

(1) Complications of the nervous system (diabetic neuropathy) : Almost 90 per cent of diabetics suffer from one or the other complication of the nervous system. However, only 25 to 50 per cent of them have to face serious complications. The most common complications of the nervous system are derangements of the touch sensation. Sometimes the touch sensation becomes abnormally acute (hyper-esthesia). The patient experiences a burning sensation in his limbs. He is more troubled during the night, when he cannot even tolerate a light covering and remains awake. At other times the touch sensation is dulled so that the patient experiences numbness in his limbs.

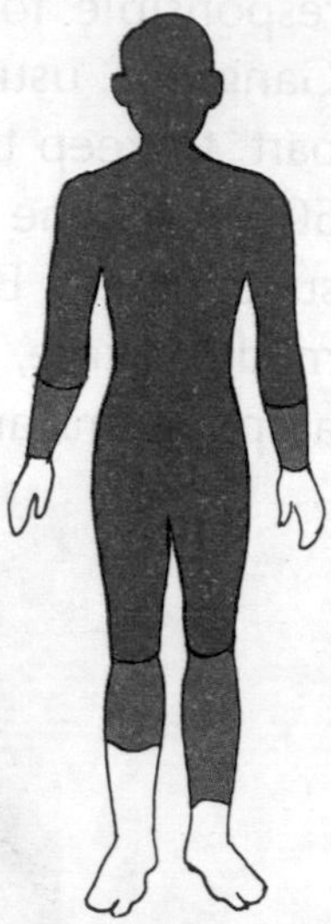

Fig. 3.3 : Derangement of the touch sensation

Undesirable effects on the autonomous nervous system bring about a decrease in the efficiency of the urinary bladder. This either leads to incomplete emptying of the bladder or uncontrollable dribbling (incontinence) of urine. When the bladder cannot be emptied completely, the retained or residual urine harbours disease causing bacteria, which leads to the inflammation of theurinary bladder (cystitis).

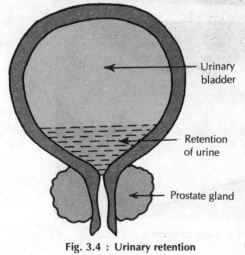

Fig. 3.4 : Urinary retention

Urinary bladder

Retention of urine

Prostate gland

(2) **Complications of the excretory system (diabetic nephropathy) :** Five years or more after the onset of diabetes, kidneys start getting harmed. About 15 per cent of diabetics succumb to some renal complication or renal failure. Diabetes gives rise to hardening of the glomeruli, the filtering units of kidneys. This condition is known as 'glomerulosclerosis'. Besides, the blood vessels of kidneys also become hard and narrow. This leads initially to loss of proteins in the urine and then gradually to a rise in blood-pressure, a swelling all over the body and kidney failure. When kidney failure ensues, serum urea and serum creatinine levels begin to rise, nausea and vomitting occurs and the patient gradually loses consciousness. The condition is usually climaxed by a total loss of consciousness (called uremic coma) which usually proves irreversible and fatal.

Diabetics more commonly suffer from an inflammation of the kidneys, called pyelonephritis.

Fig. 3.5 : Pyelonephritis

(3) **Complications of the cardiovascular system :** Diabetes speeds up the process of atherosclerosis, i.e., the degeneration of the blood vessels. In diabetics, the inner surface of blood vessels gets deposited not only with cholesterol but also with calcium. Consequently, flexible and elastic bloodvessels are transformed into hard and narrow pipes. Due to narrowing of

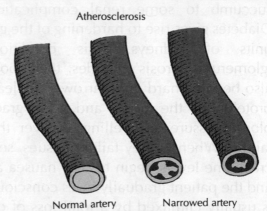

Atherosclerosis

Normal artery   Narrowed artery

Fig. 3.6 : Hardening of arteries

blood vessels, various organs of the body and the limbs do not get adequate nourishment. That is the reason why even after a short walk, a diabetic experiences pain in his calf muscles.

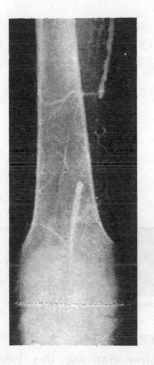

A disorder of the blood vessels of the limbs, called peripheral arterial disease, is more common in diabetics. If this disease advances too much, it may terminate in gangrene.

Due to hardening of blood vessels (atherosclerosis), the incidence of high blood pressure is very high in diabetics. Albeit, high blood pressure may also be a result of some renal complication.

Fig. 3.7 : Hardening of arteries

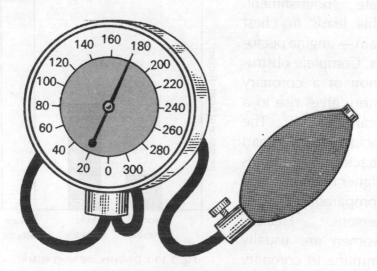

Fig. 3.8 : High blood pressure

Disorders of coronary arteries are found to be more common and more severe in diabetics. Mortality rate due to coronary artery disease is two times higher in diabetics as compared to healthy persons.

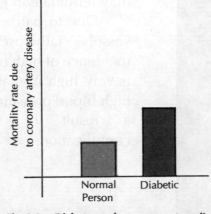

Fig. 3.9 : Diabetes and coronary artery disease

When coronary arteries become narrow, the heart cannot obtain adequate nourishment. This leads to chest pain — angina pectoris. Complete obstruction of a coronary artery gives rise to a heart attack. The incidence of heart attacks is 3 to 6 times higher in diabetics as compared to healthy persons. Healthy women are usually immune to coronary

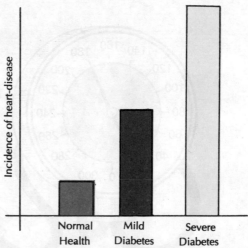

Fig. 3.10 : Diabetes and heart attack

heart disease. But incidence of heart disease in diabetic women rises to a level equal to that in men. After a heart attack, the chances for a diabetic to live for 5 more years are slim. In fact, many a diabetic succumb to the first heart attack.

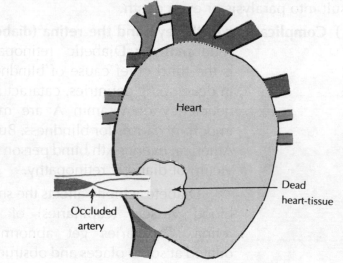

Fig. 3.11 : A heart attack

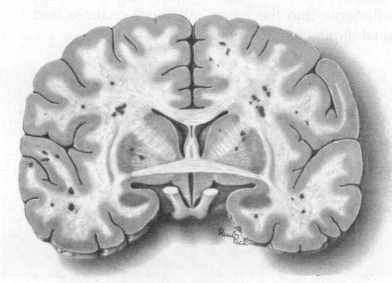

Fig. 3.12 : Cerebral haemorrhage

Degenerative changes in the arteries of a diabetic make him prone to cerebral haemorrhage. Cerebral haemorrhage may result into paralysis or even death.

(4) **Complications of the eye and the retina (diabetic retinopathy)** : Diabetic retinopathy is the third chief cause of blindness. In developing countries, cataract and deficiency of Vitamin A are more important causes for blindness. But in America, every sixth blind person is a victim of diabetic retinopathy.

Fig. 3.13 : Local dilatations of retinal capillaries

Diabetes chiefly affects the small blood vessels (capillaries) of the retina. Capillaries get abnormally dilated at some places and obstructed at other places. Degenerative changes occur in the cells of the retina. Besides, new, defective capillaries rapidly grow into the retina. All these changes lead to a gradual diminution of vision.

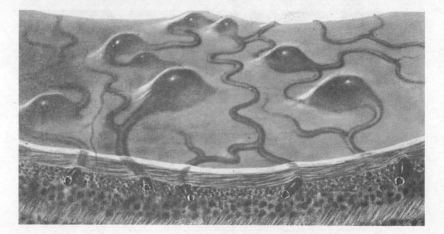

Fig. 3.14

With the progress in degenerative changes, capillaries become thinner and thinner at the sites of dilatation and may rupture, leading to retinal or vitreous haemorrhage.

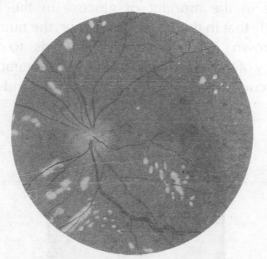

Fig. 3.15 : Retinal haemorrhage

Excessive bleeding into the retina may lead to detachment of the retina and cause sudden loss of vision.

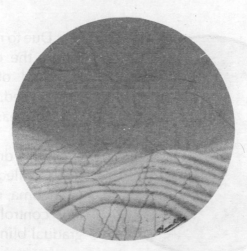

Fig. 3.16 : Retinal detachment

The crystalline lens of the eye depends for its nourishment on the glucose dissolved in the aqueous humour (a dynamic fluid present inside the eye). Due to wide fluctuations in the amount of glucose in the blood and consequently that in the aqueous humour, the nutrition of the lens is thrown into disarray. This leads to a loss in transparency of the lens. This is nothing but cataract. Diabetic cataract occurs very early in a patient's life and progresses rapidly.

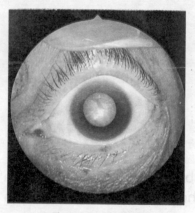

Fig. 3.17 : Cataract

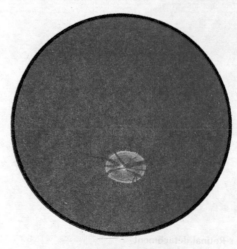

Fig. 3.18 (1) : Glaucoma

Due to neo-vascularisation, the circulation of the fluid of the eye is jeopardised. This leads to an increase in the pressure inside the eyeball, a dreadful condition called glaucoma. Glaucoma, if not adequately controlled, leads to gradual blindness.

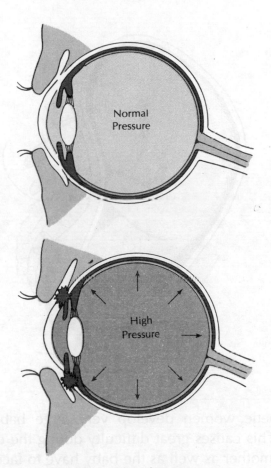

Fig. 3.18 (2) : Glaucoma

(5) Complications of the reproductive system : A diabetic woman has to face many problems during pregnancy. Diabetes creates risks to the life of the mother as well as the foetus.

About 25 per cent of pregnant diabetic women fall a victim to a dreadful condition called toxaemia of pregnancy. Toxaemia usually terminates into a miscarriage. Diabetic women more often give birth to dead babies or babies with congenital defects.

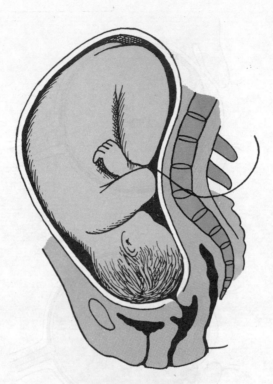

Fig. 3.19 : Still birth

Diabetic women develop very large babies in their wombs. This causes great difficulty during the delivery and both the mother as well as the baby have to face risks of an injury during delivery.

Diabetes throws the marital life of its victim into complete disarray. Diabetic women frequently suffer from frigidity and diabetic men from sexual weakness or impotence. Disorders of autonomous nervous system, too, are partly responsible for this trouble.

Fig. 3.20 : Sexual debility

(6) **Comlications of the respiratory system** : Diabetic persons easily contract infections of the respiratory tract.

About 15 per cent of patients suffering from tuberculosis are found to have diabetes. Tuberculosis and diabetes undesirably affect each other to give rise to a vicious circle of complications. Many a time, a diabetic person contracts tuber-culosis after falling a prey to diabetic coma.

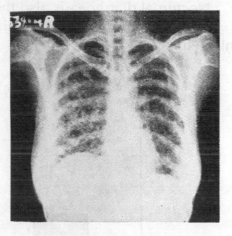

Fig. 3.21 : Pulmonary tuberculosis

Pus-filled cavities (abscesses) are formed more often in the lungs of diabetics.

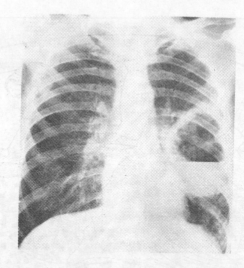

Fig. 3.22 : Lung abscess

(7) **Complications of the digestive system :** Diabetics have to face many disorders of the digestive system.

Diabetics often suffer from nausea and vomitting.

Nocturnal diarrhoea is also their common complaint.

About 25 per cent of child diabetics suffer from enlargement of the liver.

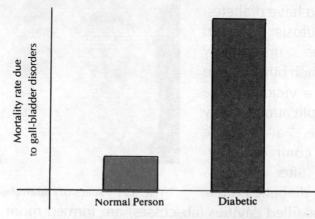

Fig. 3.23 : Diabetes and gall-bladder disorders

Gall stones are more common in diabetics. The mortality rate due to acute diseases of the gall-bladder is five times higher in diabetics than in others.

Diabetic coma arising due to defective metabolism of the dietary fats has been described earlier.

(8) **Complications of the feet :** Corns, nail infections, athlete's foot (infection of the skin between the toes), etc., are much more common in diabetics. A high blood-glucose level, a diminution in the blood-supply due to narrowing of

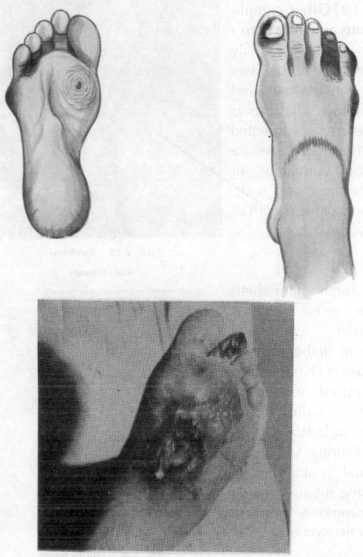

Fig. 3.24 : Diabetes and foot disorders

blood vessels and disorders of the nervous system are the factors responsible for complications of the feet.

In diabetes, even a trivial foot injury may get transformed into dreadful gangrene, which may necessitate amputation of the affected toe or the foot.

(9) Other compli-cations and infections : Diabetics easily contract skin diseases like erythrasma and moniliasis. Diabetes is sometimes suspected or detected after a person complains of infections of nails, corners of the mouth or the vagina.

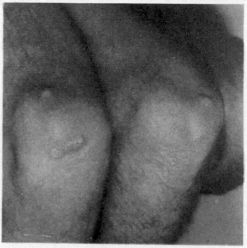

Fig. 3.25 : Xanthoma
diabeticorum

Xanthoma diabeti-corum is another disorder commonly seen in diabetics. This disease is characterised by raised red-yellow spots on palms, soles, knees or buttocks.

Pruritis valvae, a vaginal skin-disease causing intense itching is commonly seen in diabetic women.

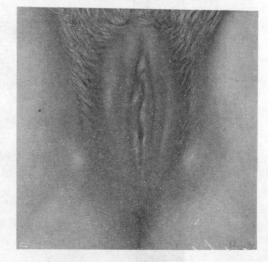

Fig. 3.26 : Pruritis valvae

Chapter in a nutshell :

1. The dreadfulness of diabetes lies in its complications.

2. Some complications can arise at any stage of the disease. Such acute or short-term complications include unconsciousness, boils, carbuncles and acute gangrene.

3. A diabetic may become unconscious under two different circumstances : when the blood-sugar level rises too high (hyperglycemia) or when the bloodsugar level plunges too low (hypoglycemia). The treatments for the two conditions are entirely different. Hence every diabetic and his near ones should know about how to distinguish between the two conditions.

4. In the long run, diabetes disrupts the functioning of almost all the systems of the body. Such chronic' complications of diabetes cannot be satisfactorily prevented even with the best treatment. Therefore, diabetes should be prevented.

4. CAUSES OF DIABETES

Diabetes was once considered a malady of the affluent society. It is no longer so. Today, diabetes makes no distinction between the rich and the poor. It strikes men as well as women, young as well as old, urbanites as well as villagers.

All the causative factors of diabetes have still not been discovered. Yet, the known factors have been discussed below :

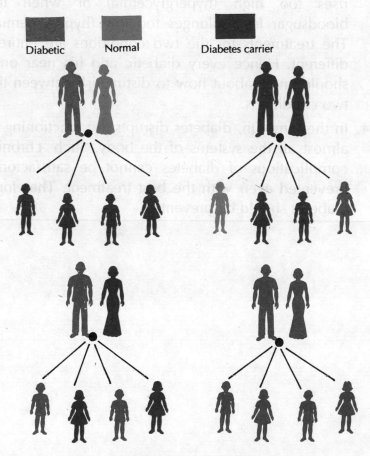

Fig. 4.1 : Heredity and diabetes – the old view

Heredity : A reference to the familial nature of diabetes can be found in ancient medical texts too. Of the total diabetics, more than 46 per cent give a family history of the disease.

There are varied opinions about how parents pass on this disease to their children. But none has been able to fully explain how heredity actually acts.

Till recent past, it was believed that the hereditary character of diabetes follows the principles of renowned geneticist Mendell, i.e., (1) If both the parents are diabetics, all their children get the disease, (2) If one of the parents is a diabetic and another is a diabetes-carrier (one who does not have the disease, but can transmit it), half the number of their children get the disease, (3) If both the parents are diabetes-carriers, one fourth the number of their children get the disease and (4) if one of the parent is a diabetic and other is healthy, their children remain free from diabetes.

However, detailed studies and surveys have proved the fallacy of this belief. It is often seen that children of diabetic parents are healthy in every respect. In identical twins one child may have diabetes and the other may remain free from the disease. Such diabetics are also seen who have no family history of the disease.

Some researchers believe that diabetes develops not because the person has inherited defective chromosome from his parents but because he has not received that chromosome from his parents, which imparts resistance to this disease.

In short, it can be said that even though hereditary factors do play a role in the development of diabetes, to what extent and in what way these factors act is still a mystery.

It can be said that hereditary factors can become effective only when certain other exciting environmental factors like obesity, faulty dietary habits and inadequate physical exertion are at work.

Obesity : It is said that, 'In diabetes, heredity loads the cannon and obesity pulls the trigger'. This saying clearly

Obesity

Weight normal : Mortality rate due to diabetes quite low

Overweight by 5 to 14 per cent : Mortality rate due to diabetes doubles

Overweight by 15 to 24 per cent : Mortality
rate due to diabetes increases fourfold

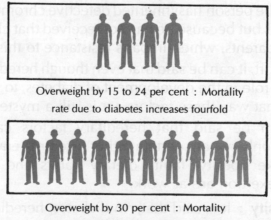

Overweight by 30 per cent : Mortality
rate due to diabetes increases tenfold

Fig. 4.2 : Obesity and diabetes

indicates the close connection between diabetes and obesity. Overweight persons become easy victims to diabetes. Studies have shown that 60 to 85 per cent of diabetics are overweight. When the second world war led to a decrease in the average weight of people, the incidence of diabetes also came down dramatically.

The more the obesity, the greater is the mortality rate due to complications of diabetes. This fact has been depicted on page 40.

Bodyweight which is 30 % below the ideal is an almost certain guarantee against diabetes. It is not an exaggeration to say that, 'Diabetes is the lawful wife of obesity'.

Incorrect dietary habits : Food can maintain or save life; it can destroy life as well. Proper food serves the purpose of medicine while improper food works as poison and causes disease.

We may take pride in calling ourselves highly civilised; but we have started to flout all the norms about the quality and quantity of food. Attracted to material pleasures, we have become slaves to our tongues. We have deleted bran from the flour; we mostly eat processed foods and refined sugar. In short, we have drifted away from mother nature, thereby initiating a rise in the incidence of diabetes. This fact is applicable to all the developing countries which have been influenced by western culture and lifestyle. According to a survey, diabetes was rare in the natives of Iceland and Canada, a few years ago. With the advent of processed and junk foods in these regions, the incidence of diabetes shot up within a very short time.

By offering chocolates, cakes and icecreams too often to our children, by giving the refrigerator a place in our homes and by attending parties every other day, we in fact invite obesity and diabetes.

For the origin of diabetes, excessive food is as much to be blamed as improper (i.e., refined and processed) food. The body has to produce more digestive juices and insulin to digest excessive food. Under the pressure of such excessive work-load, the pancreas gland weakens and ultimately breaks down, leading to diabetes. A philosopher has rightly said that, 'Very few people die of starvation; the rest die of overeating' It would not be an exaggeration to say that we dig our graves with our teeth.

Many a renowned researcher holds the belief that a deficiency of vitamin B_6 (pyridoxine) in our diet may also be a cause of diabetes. Lack of Vitamin B_6 causes the transformation of tryptophane (an amino-acid present in our diet) into xanthurenic acid which harms the beta cells of the pancreas to cause diabetes. If experimental animals are fed with a vitamin B_6 deficient diet, pancreatic destruction starts within 48 hours and symptoms of diabetes show up. A similar result can be obtained by injecting xanthurenic acid into the bodies of animals. If the pancreas is not completely damaged, large doses of vitamin B_6 can reverse the symptoms of diabetes. Experiments have also shown that treatment with the mineral magnesium too produces similarly celubrious effects on experimentally damaged pancreases.

Consumption of food containing excessive animal proteins, saturated fats and calories also stimulates the production of xanthurenic acid inside the body. A similar effect is produced by the penicillin group of drugs.

Some researchers believe that diabetes arises not because of inheriting defective chromosome but because of genetically determined excessive requirement of vitamin B_6. Of course, further research and investigations are called for to validate this belief.

Inadequate physical work : Because of the industrialisation, man has drifted away from physical labour. Sedentary life, too, plays an important role in the origin of diabetes. During physical work, muscles use up a lot of glucose present in the blood. Consequently, the work-load on the pancreas is reduced. Moreover, physical labour also prevents or reduces obesity, which is intimately connected with diabetes.

Viral infection : A possible role of some viral infection as an aetiological factor for diabetes is also being considered by many a scientist. Some children have been seen to contract diabetes after suffering from mumps, a viral infection. The viruses destroy the insulin-producing beta cells of the pancreas. Besides, the antibodies produced by the body to fight the virus also attack the beta cells and aggravate the disease.

Effects of certain hormones : Some harmones produced in the body have an action opposite to that of insulin, i.e., they increase the amount of glucose in the blood. Such hormones include glucagon, cortisone, growth hormone, adrenaline and thyroxine. If the secretion of these hormones is excessive, the effectiveness of efficiency of insulin decreases and blood glucose level rises.

Fig. 4.3 : Mental tension

Side-effects of certain drugs : Long-term use of certain drugs like cortisone (used for asthma, respiratory diseases, arthritis and skin-diseases), contraceptive pills and thyroid group of drugs can also produce diabetes by harming the pancreas.

Other illnesses : Acute pancreatitis, a heart attack or some other illnesses may precipitate diabetes. This fact is more applicable to persons who are carriers of diabetes or who have a family-history of diabetes. In such persons, an acute illness may unmask latent diabetes. Acute pancreatitis is an important cause of diabetes in Kerala and South Africa.

Psychological factors : Acute emotional upset, shock or mental stress may unmask latent diabetes. However, this factor plays a greater role in enhancing established diabetes than in actually causing this disease.

Chapter in a nutshell :

1. Once diabetes was a malady of the affluent class. Today, however, it makes no distinction between the rich and the poor, a man or a woman, the young and the old, a city-dweller or a villager. The incidence of diabetes is rising at an alarming pace in our country.

2. Heredity is an important aetiological factor in diabetes. However, the mechanism of its action is still not clear.

3. The siblings of diabetic parents do possess the seed of the disease. The seed, however, cannot develop into a plant unless nurtured by environmental factors like obesity, faulty dietary habits, a sedentary life-style and negative thinking. Thus in diabetes, heredity loads the cannon and environmental factors (e.g., obesity, excessive food-intake, etc.) pull the trigger.

4. It is also believed that diabetes is caused by a viral infection.

5. SYMPTOMS OF DIABETES

Diabetes is a great mimic. It affects various organs or systems of the body to give rise to such symptoms as would sometimes mislead even a physician.

Maturity onset diabetes creeps into the body so silently that the victim usually remains unaware and symptomless. On the other hand, juvenile diabetes develops suddenly and gives rise to dramatic symptoms.

Symptoms : The following symptoms point towards a possibility of diabetes :

(1) **Polyurea (excessive and frequent urination) :** The sugar escaping in the urine, drags along with itself, a large quantity of water. A diabetic, therefore, frequently passes large amounts of urine.

(2) **Polydipsia (dryness of mouth and excessive thirst) :** This symptom is the result of efforts by the body to compensate for the fluids lost through excessive urine.

(3) **Polyphagia (excessive hunger) :** In diabetes, glucose cannot enter the various body-cells. Thus the cells starve in spite of being bathed by the glucose-rich serum. They suffer from 'poverty in the midst of plenty'. To overcome this cellular starvation, the body gives rise to abnormal and excessive hunger.

(4) **Loss of weight :** When the cells cannot utilise glucose, the body disintegrates stored fats to provide the cells with the necessary nourishment. Therefore, the person loses weight.

(5) **Weakness, fatigue and body-ache :** The body also disintegrates stored muscle-protein to nourish the starving cells. This is the cause of undue weakness and fatigue.

(6) **Mental fatigue and lack of concentration :** The brain-cells have to depend chiefly on glucose for their nourishment. However, they cannot utilize the available glucose, due to which the person experiences undue mental fatigue, cannot concentrate and becomes forgetful.

(7) **Wound-infection and delayed healing :** Glucose-rich blood is a good breeding medium for pus-forming micro-organisms. Moreover, diabetes also affects the small bloodvessels (micro-angiopathy) and nerves (neuropathy) leading to a decrease in the blood-supply of the skin and derangement of skin-sensations. That is the reason why even a small wound on a diabetic person's body easily gets infected and fails to heal in time.

(8) **Easy susceptibility to infections of the skin, gums and the respiratory system :** The glucose-rich blood of a diabetic provides optimum conditions for a rapid growth and reproduction of disease-causing micro-organisms. Besides, the hormonal imbalance causes a decrease in the natural resistance power of the body against disease. Hence a diabetic easily contracts infections of the skin, gums and the respiratory tract. He commonly suffers from boils, carbuncles, pyorrhoea, cough and colds.

(9) **Intense itching all over the body, especially that of the genital parts :** Many a time, diabetes is suspected and later diagnosed in women complaining of intense itching of the genital parts. Irritation of the nerve-endings on the skin and on the genital organs due to excessive glucose in the blood is the cause for this trouble.

(10) **Frequent changes in the sharpness of vision and the spectacle-numbers :** Changes in the glucose con-centration of the internal fluid (aqueous) of the eyes leads to variations in their focussing power. That is the reason why a diabetic has to often change his spectacle lenses. The crystalline lens of the eye depends, for its nourishment and transparency, on the glucose dissolved in the aqueous. In

diabetes, the nourishment of the crystalline lens is jeopardised, leading to an untimely cataract.

(11) Aching or numbness of limbs and an abnormal increase or decrease in skin-sensations : Diabetes untowardly affects the whole nervous system to give rise to these symptoms.

(12) Sexual debility or impotence : General weakness, disintegration of muscle-protein, mental depression and undesirable changes in the blood-circulatory and nervous systems give rise to these symptoms.

(13) Diabetic unconsciousness (hyperglycemic coma) : As stated earlier, the body disintegrates stored fats to nourish starving cells. Fat disintegration leads to the production of ketone bodies in the blood. Excessive increase of ketone bodies makes the blood acidic and gradually leads to unconsciousness. Many a time, diabetes is suspected or diagnosed after the victim becomes unconscious.

Besides, following circumstances should also arouse suspicion of diabetes :

(1) Sudden weight-gain after the age of 45 years.

(2) Coronary heart disease.

(3) Cerebral haemorrage.

The symptoms of diabetes described in this chapter are observed in only about 30 per cent of diabetics. In others, especially during the earlier stages of the disease, there are no symptoms and the disease is diagnosed due to a presenting complication or accidentally, e. g. –

(1) During a general check-up for some other disease.

(2) During laboratory investigations prior to some surgery.

(3) During investigations advised by a Life Insurance Corporation.

The investigations, which lead to the diagnosis of diabetes, have been described in the next chapter.

Chapter in a nutshell :

1. Juvenile diabetes gives rise to acute and dramatic symptoms. It is characterised by a triad of symptoms : excessive thirst (polydipsia), excessive hunger (polyphagia) and excessive urination (polyurea).

2. Maturity onset diabetes produces no symptoms, at least not in its early stage. It is usually diagnosed accidentally, through investigations performed for some other complaint.

3. Other symptoms of diabetes include general lassitude, undue fatigue, frequent boils, deranged sensations of the limbs, delayed wound-healing, sexual debility and unconsciousness.

6. DIAGNOSIS OF DIABETES

Diabetes is first detected under various circumstances.

The symptoms of acute diabetes are so dramatic that it is almost impossible to miss the diagnosis. But in a number of patients, diabetes develops so gradually and silently that it is revealed only by the methodical examination of the urine and the blood. It is believed that undiagnosed diabetics probably outnumber known diabetics.

It is precisely for this reason that all persons above 35 years of age, especially if they are obese or have a family history of diabetes, should get their urine and blood examined at regular intervals of time, to ascertain the presence or absence of diabetes. Actually most of these tests are utterly simple and can be learnt or performed by every interested person.

Diagnostic investigations :

(A) Tests to detect the presence of sugar in the urine (glycosuria) :

(1) Benedict's Test : This is a very simple and effective method of ascertaining the presence or the amount of glucose in the urine and can be done by the diabetic himself.

Apparatus :

Benedict's solution (fresh; certainly not more than 3 months old),

Dropper,

Test-tube,

Test-tube holder.

Procedure :

Take 5 ml. (one teaspoon) of Benedict's solution in the test-tube.

Holding the test-tube with the holder, heat it over a spirit lamp till the Benedict's solution boils without overflowing.

3 / Diabetes......Without Any Fear

Drop 8 to 10 drops of urine into the boiling Benedict's solution.

After again boiling the mixture, let it cool down.

While cooling, the mixture changes colour.

The colour of the mixture serves as a guide to the amount of sugar in the urine : blue – sugar absent; green – 0·5 % sugar; yellow – 1 % sugar; orange – 1·5 % sugar; brick red – 2 % or more sugar.

The concentration of sugar in the urine can also be judged by matching the colour of the urine with one of the colours given below :

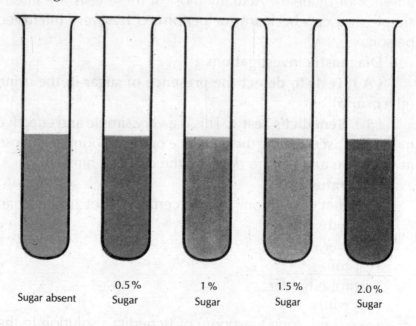

| Sugar absent | 0.5 %
Sugar | 1 %
Sugar | 1.5 %
Sugar | 2.0 %
Sugar |

Fig. 6.1 : The amount of sugar in the urine

Note : It is essential that the above test be performed two hours after a meal. In the initial stages of the disease, a diabetic does not lose sugar in his urine, when on empty stomach. Hence if the Benedict's test is performed in the fasting state, it is possible to miss the diagnosis of the disease.

Even if sugar is detected in the urine by Benedict's test, the diagnosis of diabetes should be confirmed by blood-analysis. Sometimes sugar may overflow into the urine even without its concentration being high in the blood. This is a benign condition, termed 'renal glycosuria'. ·

Thus Benedict's test does not have a diagnostic significance. It is more important to ascertain the degree of control of the disease, in a person who is undergoing treatment.

Efforts have been made to devise tests simpler than this test. One such test is 'clinitest'. Clinitest tablets are available in the market. First, a mixture of 5 drops of urine and 10 drops of water is taken in a test-tube. A clinitest tablet, when dropped into the test-tube, makes the mixture boil on its own. The hot mixture gradually changes colour. A colour-chart provided with the tablets can be used to match the colour of the urine and hence judge the amount of sugar present.

The note given below the Benedict's test is applicable to clinitest too.

(2) **Glucose oxidase test :** Paper or plastic strips, called diastix or tes-tape are available in the market. A colour-chart is provided along with the strips. While passing urine two hours after a meal, the person has to hold a tes-tape or a diastix strip in the urine-stream for a few moments. The

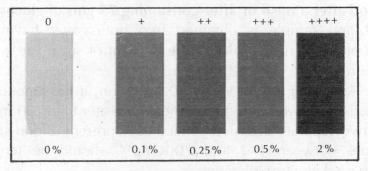

Fig. 6.3 : The amount of sugar in the urine

strip changes colour on coming in contact with the urine. After 30 to 60 seconds the colour of the strip should be matched with one of the colours of the provided chart to assess the amount of sugar in the urine.

Both the above tests are more simple and sensitive than Benedict's test; but they are somewhat expensive. They are very useful to a person who is away from home.

The note given below Benedict's test is applicable to glucose oxidase test as well.

(B) Tests to detect the amount of sugar in the blood : It should be noted that a certain amount of sugar is always present in the blood and necessarily so. In diabetes, the blood-sugar level rises above the normal or physiological limits.

(1) Fasting blood sugar : A sample of the blood is obtained when the person is in a fasting state and the amount of sugar is assessed.

This test alone is not adequate for the diagnosis of diabetes because in early or mild diabetes, the blood-sugar values may be normal in the fasting state. Thus a diagnosis of diabetes may be missed.

However, if the amount of blood-sugar in the fasting state is found to be greater than 140 mg% on two separate occasions, it is a sure indication of diabetes.

(2) Post-prandial blood sugar (amount of sugar in the blood after a meal or after consuming 75 gms of glucose) : A blood sample is obtained two hours after having a carbohydrate-rich meal and the amount of sugar present is determined.

According to the W. H. O. criterion, if the amount of blood-sugar two hours after a meal is greater than 200 mg% on two separate occasions, diabetes is present. Blood-sugar values between 140 and 200 mg% should be termed 'impaired glucose tolerance'.

This is a more reliable test to diagnose diabetes than fasting blood-sugar estimation.

(3) **Glucose tolerance test** : This is a superb test to evaluate the metabolism of dietary carbohydrates in the body.

Certain precautions should be taken before undergoing this test.

During the three days preceding the test, the person should eat a carbohydrate-rich diet. During this period, cortisone group of drugs and other drugs like nicotinic acid, vitamin C, aspirin, thiazide diuretics and oral contraceptives should not be taken.

After taking the evening meal on the day prior to the test-day, the person should not eat or drink anything. He should not even smoke. On the test-day, the person should go for the test early in the morning, with an empty stomach.

First of all, urine and blood samples are collected to determine fasting urine-sugar and blood-sugar. The person is then given to drink a solution containing 75 to 100 gms of glucose and a few drops of lemon juice. Thereafter, blood and urine samples are obtained every half an hour, for the next $2\frac{1}{2}$ hours and analysed for the amount of sugar. On the basis of these findings, the efficiency of the body to metabolise dietary glucose is known.

The following characteristics are seen in a healthy person during this test :

(1) Fasting blood-sugar level is less than 120 mg% (many a time 100 mg %).

(2) The amount of glucose in the blood rises to a maximum value in 30 to 60 minutes after the meal. This maximum value is not more than 160 mg%.

(3) Two hours after the meal, the blood-glucose level comes down to the fasting level.

Diabetics, on the other hand, show the following characteristics during this test :

(1) Fasting blood-sugar level is equal to or greater than 140 mg %. However, in early or mild diabetes the value obtained may be a little lower, say 120 mg %.

(2) After the meal, the concentration of blood-sugar takes more than an hour to reach the maximum value. This maximum value is equal to or greater than 200 mg % (W.H.O. criterion). However in early or mild diabetes the maximum value obtained may be 180 mg %.

(3) Two hours after the meal, the amount of blood-glucose is still quite high (140 mg % or more) as compared to normal.

The above-mentioned normal and abnormal values of blood-glucose have been tabulated below :

	Blood glucose concentration (in mg)		
	Fasting Value	Maximum Value	Value two hours after consuming glucose
Normal	less than 120	less than 160	less than 120
Early (borderline) diabetes	120 to 140	160 to 180	120 to 140
Established diabetes	more than 140	200 or more	more than 140

The graph, plotted on the basis of blood-sugar values obtained during glucose tolerance test, is called 'glucose tolerance curve'.

Normal and diabetic glucose tolerance curves have been depicted below :

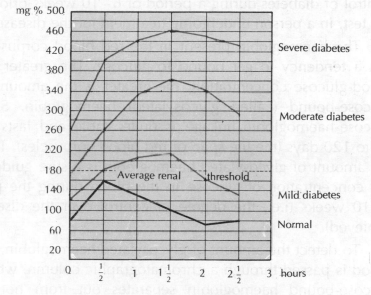

Fig. 6.3 : Glucose tolerance curve

(4) Stress (steroid primed) glucose tolerance test : This test is more important to detect prediabetes or latent diabetes. The logic behind this test is that if persons with a possibility of developing diabetes in future (especially those having a family history of the disease) are given, besides glucose, a steroid drug like cortisone (50 mg) or prednisone (10 mg) or triamcilone (8 mg), a physical state resembling diabetes develops; such a diabetes-like state cannot be developed in healthy persons even with steroid drugs.

The procedure of this test is exactly similar to that of glucose tolerance test. After the person consumes 75 gms of glucose and the steroid drug (in above-mentioned amount), blood samples are periodically drawn from his body. If the blood sugar is 160 mg or more after one hour or 140 mg or more after two hours, the person may be considered to be in a prediabetic or latent–diabetes state and may develop frank diabetes in the future.

(5) **Glycosylated haemoglobin test :** This test is not important to detect diabetes. It is more important to judge the control of diabetes during a period of 6 – 10 weeks prior to the test, in a person undergoing treatment for the disease.

The haemoglobin present in the red blood corpuscles has a tendency to get bound to glucose. The greater the blood-glucose concentration, the greater is the amount of glucose-bound (called glycosylated) haemoglobin. Such glucose-haemoglobin linkage is quite stable and lasts for 60 to 120 days (the life-span of red blood corpuscles). Thus the amount of glycosylated haemoglobin is a sure guide to the concentration of glucose in the blood during the past 6 – 10 weeks (i.e., the degree of control over the disease achieved).

To detect the amount of glycosylated haemoglobin, the blood is passed through a chromatographic column, where glucose-bound haemoglobin separates out from normal haemoglobin. Normal and abnormal values of glycosylated haemoglobin have been given below.

	Amount of glycosylated haemoglobin	Control of diabetes
1	6 to 8%	excellent
2	8 to 10%	good
3	10 to 12%	satisfactory
4	Above 12%	unsatisfactory

This test is most important for pregnant diabetic women because uncontrolled diabetes may risk the lives of the mother and the child; therefore ignorance about the degree of control of the disease is undesirable.

Other investigations which may help the diabetic : Laboratory investigations are inevitable to assess the degree of control achieved while treating diabetes. Of such investigations urine-sugar estimation is the most common and important investigation.

Besides, there are other investigations which help to detect complications of diabetes. These include the estimation of acetone, albumin and chlorides in urine.

The presence of acetone in the urine is an indication of ketosis. On detection of acetone, rapid steps should be taken to prevent diabetic coma.

The presence of albumin in the urine is an indication that something is wrong with either kidneys or the ureter.

The estimation of the amounts of chlorides in urine gives information about the state of electrolyte-balance in the diabetic's body.

Rothera's Test for acetone :

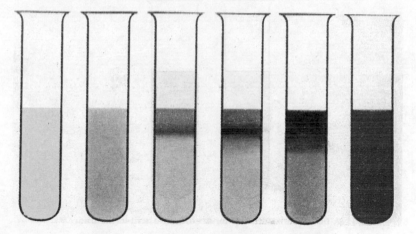

Fig. 6.4 : Rothera's test for acetone in the urine

(1) Take a test-tube. Fill up a third of it by solid ammonium sulphate.

(2) Add 5 ml of urine to the test-tube.

(3) Add 8 – 10 drops of 0·25 % sodium nitroprusside solution.

(4) Finally add to the test-tube, 1 – 2 ml of concentrated ammonia solution.

Presence of acetone or aceto-acetic acid in the urine is indicated by permanganate–like purple colouration of contents of the test-tube.

Gerhardt's test for aceto-acetic acid :

(1) Take 5 ml urine in a test-tube.

(2) Add to it, drop by drop, a 3% ferric chloride solution. A white precipitate of ferric phosphate will be formed.

(3) Add some more ferric chloride and filter the contents of the test-tube through a filter paper.

A purple or dark brown colouration of the filterate indicates the presence of aceto-acetic acid in the urine.

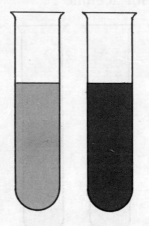

Fig. 6.5 : Gerhardt's test for aceto-acetic acid in the urine

Sulphosalicylic test for albumin :

(1) Filter the urine.

(2) Take 1 ml urine in a test tube.

(3) Add to it 1 ml of sulphosalicylic acid (concentration : 30 gms in 100 ml).

(4) Let the mixture stand for 10 minutes.

A milky or cloudy appearance of the mixture indicates the presence of albumin; a clear solution is an indication of its absence.

Another test for albumin :

(1) Fill up 2 / 3 of the test-tube with urine.

(2) Drop a red litmus paper into the test-tube. If the urine is alkaline it will turn the litmus paper blue. Now add to the test-tube, 10 % acetic acid drop by drop. After every drop, shake the test-tube vigorously. Stop adding acetic acid as soon as the litmus paper is seen to turn red.

(3) Now hold the test-tube slightly inclined and heat the upper part of the mixture on a spirit lamp.

(4) A cloudy or milky appearance of the mixture indicates the presence of either albumin or phosphates.

(5) To the milky mixture, add 10 % acetic acid drop by drop. Simultaneously, heat the test-tube. Disappearance of the milkiness is an indication of phosphates and persistence of milkiness is an indication of albumin in the urine.

Test for chlorides :

(1) Take 25 ml of urine in the test-tube.

(2) Slowly add to it, 10 drops of concentrated nitric acid.

(3) Finally add 2 – 3 ml of 3 % silver nitrate solution.

Normally a curd-like white precipitate forms in the test-tube. If the electrolyte-balance inside the body is disrupted, the amount of chlorides in urine decreases. Then the white precipitate does not form (or forms very slightly).

Chapter in a nutshell :

1. Many investigations are available to diagnose diabetes.

2. Benedict's test to detect the presence (or absence) of sugar in the urine is extremely simple and should be learnt by every diabetic. Even when sugar has been found to be present in the urine, the diagnosis of diabetes should be confirmed by blood-sugar estimation.

3. If the concentration of sugar in the blood, two hours after a carbohydrate-rich meal, is greater than 140 mg%, the diagnosis of diabetes is confirmed.

4. Glucose tolerance test (GTT) is considered to be the best test to detect diabetes. In this test, the person is first made to consume a carbohydrate-rich meal (or 75 – 100 gms of glucose) and thereafter samples of his blood are withdrawn at half-hourly intervals and the blood-sugar levels estimated.

5. The likelihood of a person developing diabetes in future can be predicted with the help of stress (steroid primed) glucose tolerance test.

6. Glycosylated haemoglobin test can help to judge the degree of control over the disease, achieved during the past two months.

7. Persons with a family-history of diabetes should, after the age of 35, regularly get their urine and blood examined, even if no symptoms of the disease present themselves.

7. TREATMENT OF DIABETES

Considering the present medical knowledge, it can be said that diabetes is a life-time disease. With intelligent treatment, it can be kept under complete control and some of its complications prevented. But a permanent cure still remains elusive. Thus the treatment of diabetes is a life-time responsibility.

Some diabetics, on knowledge of their disease, resign themselves to fate. 'Now that the disease has developed and death is a certainty, I should thoroughly enjoy myself for the rest of life', is their misguided belief. They throw all the health-rules to the wind and indulge in excesses. But to man, death is not available for the asking. When dreadful complications of the disease overpower such careless or happy-go-lucky persons, life becomes miserable and intolerable. Ignoring the treatment of diabetes is like axing one's own feet.

The treatment of diabetes does not rob a person of worldly pleasures or make his life dreary. In fact, a person undergoing treatment can lead an almost normal life.

Aims of treatment :

(1) To ameliorate all the symptoms of the disease,

(2) To control the concentration of blood-glucose,

(3) To prevent glucose from escaping in the urine,

(4) To formulate a 'whole-day diet-plan' such that all the essential nutrients are available to the body. In child diabetics, the diet should be enough to encourage physical development. Another thing to be kept in mind while planning the diet is that the body-weight is to be brought to the ideal level,

(5) To convince the person of the importance of regular physical exercise and to formulate an exercise-programme as per the individual needs,

(6) To educate the diabetic (and also his family members, if possible) about different aspects of the disease and its treatment.

The last point needs further elucidation. In the treatment of diabetes, the patient has to bear an almost equal (perhaps greater) responsibility, as compared to the attending physician. He can intelligently and successfully shoulder this responsibility only if he is aware of all the facts of the disease. However, because of several limitations, especially those of time, no doctor can educate his patient fully. That is precisely the reason for bringing out this book.

Modes of treatment :

Diabetes can be treated through –

1. Diet, 2. Exercise, 3. Medicines, 4. Acupuncture/ Acupressure and 5. Magnet Therapy.

1. Diet

[**Note :** In the treatment of diabetes, diet is of utmost importance. Hence we have discussed it in detail here.]

'A true doctor first tries to treat the disease by food; only when food fails does he prescribe medicines.' This excellent advice given by Sun Semiao, an early Chinese medical writer of the 6th century, holds good in the treatment of diabetes even today.

Diet is the single most important factor in the successful treatment of diabetes. In spite of all the advances in the field of medical treatment, diet has maintained its supremacy. If faulty dietary habits are persisted with, drugs cannot help. Besides, for obese diabetics, a dietary change is the only treatment of choice.

Principles of diet-planning :

A diabetic's diet should be such as would –

(1) supply in sufficient amounts, energy-giving nutrients like carbohydrates, proteins and fats,

(2) supply in sufficient amounts, vitamins and minerals which are necessary for the body and for the control of diabetes,

(3) supply enough calories (nutrition) to the body to attain or maintain ideal body-weight.

(4) help in avoiding or controlling complications of diabetes.

Total quantity of food : It is generally agreed that during the course of a day, a diabetic should be given food that would supply about 30 calories per ideal body-weight. However, whether the diabetic has to do a manual or a sedentary job and whether he is overweight or underweight should be considered while deciding the whole-day rationing of food. A general rule has been tabulated below :

	Sedentary life	Moderate physical activity	Severe physical activity
Obese diabetic	20 – 25 cal/kg	30 cal/kg	35 cal/kg
Shapely diabetic	30 cal/kg	35 cal/kg	40 cal/kg
Lean diabetic	35 cal/kg	40 cal/kg	45 – 50 cal/kg

A diet supplying 1500 to 1800 calories during the day would be sufficient for a middle-aged and sedentary diabetic.

However, developing children, pregnant women, breast-feeding mothers and sportsmen would need more food.

The total food should be consumed in four or five almost equal parts during the day. Many diabetics commit the mistake of taking only two meals a day. Naturally, such meals are heavy. The insulin produced in the body (or that injected as a medicine) is insufficient to metabolise this excessive food. Hence the blood sugar level rises. On the other hand, at a time midway between two meals, the glucose level drops down abnormally. Such wide fluctuations of blood-glucose levels are undesirable. Besides, if the blood-glucose concentration drops down too much, it may lead to a hypoglycemic coma, a critical condition. It is therefore advisable for the diabetic to have 4 to 5 small meals equally spaced out during the day.

How the total allowance of calories should be obtained in parts has been suggested below :

About 20% of the total calories through the morning breakfast,

About 40% of the total calories through the lunch,

About 10% of the total calories through the afternoon tea-coffee and snacks,

About 20% of the total calories through the dinner,

The rest 10% of the total calories through late evening milk and snacks/fruits.

The diet : 'What type of diet should a diabetic take?' is an important question which calls for a detailed answer.

It is a sad fact that a diabetic does not get adequate guidance about food. Most advices about diet are limited to prohibiting or curtailing the use of refined sugar, jaggery, rice, potatoes and fried eatables. In fact, besides the things to be avoided, a diabetic should also be supplied with a list of things to be eaten, the right amounts of those foods and the proper timings for taking those foods. Half knowledge does more harm than good to the diabetic because apart from the prohibited 4 or 5 items of food, he continues to eat everything else, thereby inviting a rise in blood-glucose level.

Some diabetics, heeding to the advice of their relatives or friends, observe fasts or opt for fad diets consisting of one or two food articles (e.g., chapaties and cooked karela; chapaties and leafy vegetables, etc.). This gradually leads to depletion of vitamins and minerals stored in the body and gives rise to symptoms of their deficiency. Besides, sooner or later, the tongue rebels against such monotonous diet. Ultimately the diabetic develops such aversion to dieting that he reverts to old faulty food-habits with a vengeance. In fact, a diabetic can choose his diet from a variety of food-articles. He need not stay away from the tastes he likes. Similarly he need not consume diet which is entirely different from that prepared for the rest of his family. Wheat, rice or bajri are similar in their nutrient contents. Likewise most vegetables have similar nutrients. Thus there is no reason why a diabetic should eat the same cereal or the same vegetable day after day.

The major constituents of the food we eat are : carbohydrates, proteins, fats, vitamins, minerals and fibres (roughage). To maintain health and to aid the various processes occurring in the body, it is essential that all these constituents are obtained in sufficient amount.

Carbohydrates include sugar and starch. Cereals are their main sources. Refined sugar, jaggery, honey, etc. are concentrated forms of carbohydrates. One gram of carbohydrates provides energy worth 4 calories to the body.

Proteins are essential for the growth of the body and regeneration of cells lost due to wear and tear. Milk, pulses, meat, fish and eggs are their main sources. One gram of protein provides energy worth 4 calories to the body.

Fats are available from ghee and oils. There are two types of fat : saturated and unsaturated. Saturated fats are believed to be the causes of narrowing and hardening of arteries (atherosclerosis). Atherosclerosis ultimately leads to a heart attack or cerebral haemorrhage. It is therefore desirable to drastically cut down the consumption of food articles containing saturated fats. Butter, ghee, vegetable ghee, coconut oil and palm oil have lots of saturated fats. Meat, fish and eggs too are rich in saturated fats. On the other hand, groundnut oil, til oil, corn oil, soyabean oil, linseed oil and cotton seed oil are sources of relatively harmless, unsaturated fats. Each gram of fat provides energy worth 9 calories to the body.

Vitamins and minerals are extremely important nutrients which serve numerous functions inside the body. Raw vegetables, fruits, germinated pulses and germinated cereals are excellent sources of vitamins and minerals.

During the past 60–65 years the notions about the proportions of carbohydrates, proteins and fats in a diabetic diet have undergone a radical change.

Uptil the second decade of this century, diabetics were advised to consume a very low-carbohydrate and very high-fat diet. But gradually it became known that a high-fat diet ruins the blood vessels and harms the heart. Besides, no logical reason could be put forward for carbohydrate–restriction. Modern dieticians and physicians recommend, for the diabetics, a diet 55 to 60 per cent of which is comprised of carbohydrates, 20 to 22 per cent of fats and 18–20 per cent of proteins.

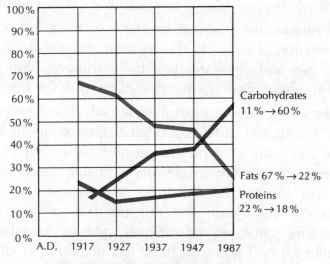

Fig. 7.1 : The change in the notions about diabetic food during the past 70 years

It is now unanimously agreed that a diabetic should receive a larger than usual quota of vitamins and minerals.

In chapter 4 it was mentioned that some researchers have propounded the 'Vit B_6 deficiency and diabetes' theory. According to their view, lack of vitamin B_6 raises the xanthurenic acid content of the blood, which in turn damages the pancreas and leads to diabetes. A fact which supports this belief is that all diabetics excrete large amounts of xanthurenic acid in their urine. If diabetics are given 50 mg of vitamin B_6 every day, urinary xanthurenic acid rapidly diminishes and symptoms of diabetes begin to disappear. [1, 2] Dr. Rosen has recommended that every diabetic should be given at least 10 mg of vitamin B_6 daily.

Magnesium has been found to bring down the requirements of vitamin B_6 by decreasing the xanthurenic content of the body. Dieticians suggest that every diabetic should receive 500 mg of magnesium daily. [3, 4, 5]

Some researchers claim that Vitamin C, Vitamin B_1 and panthothenic acid are helpful to diabetics because, like sulphonurea drugs, they stimulate the pancreas to produce more insulin. [6, 7, 8] Again, animals kept on a totally 'Vitamin C-free' diet manufacture less insulin in their bodies and develop symptoms similar to those of diabetes. [9, 10]

It has been seen that diabetics given 300 to 600 units of vitamin E daily, many a time require much smaller doses of medicinal insulin. [11, 12]

Chemical analysis has also shown that diabetics suffer from a vitamin A deficiency[13]. Experiments have shown that when diabetics are daily given about 15000 to 16000 units of vitamin A, their health improves and the concentration of cholesterol in their blood falls.[14]

Chromium is also a very important mineral for diabetics. If there is chromium deficiency in the body, the effectivity of insulin decreases. If experimental animals are made chromium deficient, their blood-glucose and blood-cholesterol levels rise.[15]

In short, a diabetic's requirements of vitamins and minerals are much greater than normal. The natural sources of these vitamins and minerals have been enlisted in the appendices given at the end of this book. Besides, if a need arises, these vitamins and minerals can be obtained through pills as well.

It is desirable that the fibre-content of our diet is high. People or tribes who give fibre-containing food articles a due place in their diet, almost always succeed in keeping diabetes and other diseases at bay. Africans are living proofs of this fact.

If a diet is rich in fibres, the absorption of glucose through the intestines is slowed down. Consequently the blood-sugar level rises gradually. The pancreas gland is able to cope with such a situation very easily. Dr. James Anderson of Cantucky University has proved through experiments that when diabetics are given a high-fibre diet, their medicinal insulin requirements are reduced by almost 25 per cent. Vegetables, fruits, whole cereals and whole pulses are excellent sources of fibres. By removing bran from the flour, by eating polished rice, by keeping away from fruits-vegetables and by consuming processed, refined and soft foods, we invite not only diabetes but also other diseases, right from constipation to cancer.

Daily diet-plan : On the basis of the abovesaid facts, a diet for the whole day can easily be planned.

Of the total 1500 to 1800 calories–

(1) 900 to 1075 calories should be obtained through carbohydrates. For this the amount of carbohydrates required will be 225 to 275 gms.

(2) 325 to 400 calories should be obtained through fats. For this the amount of fats required wil be 35 to 45 gms.

(3) 275 to 325 calories should be obtained through proteins. For this the amount of proteins required will be 70 to 80 gms.

The carbohydrate, fat and protein – contents of various foods have been enlisted in appendices given at the end of the book.

At the outset, a diabetic should first clearly understand what foods he can take freely, what foods should be taken in moderation and what foods should be totally avoided. The following list will guide him in this respect :

Prohibited foods : Sugar, glucose, honey, jam, chocolates, sweets, sweet drinks, sweetened milk, canned fruits, sweet biscuits, cakes, pie, pudding, peppermint and alcohol.

Foods to be taken in moderation : Cereals, pulses, potatoes, peas, dry fruits, cheese, milk, butter, ghee, oil, meat, eggs, fish.

Food that can be taken as desired : Most fruits, vegetables, drinks (tea, coffee, etc. sweetened with sachharine).

Classification of foods :

Foods can be divided into eight categories :

(1) **Vegetables (Type A) :** e.g., cabbage, cauli flower, cucumber, brinjals, karelas, ladies fingers, tomatoes, raddish, chillies, etc.

The carbohydrate – content of these vegetables is very low. Such vegetables can be taken as much as desired in the raw form; however they should not be consumed more than a cupful if cooked.

(2) **Vegetables (Type B) :** e.g., carrots, onion, green peas, beet, raw mangoes, etc.

Every 100 gms ($\frac{1}{2}$ cup) of these vegetables have 7 gms of carbohydrates and 2 gms of proteins (totally 36 calories).

(3) **Fruits :** The following fruits, when consumed in quantities mentioned alongside, supply 10 gms of carbohydrates (i.e. 40 calories) :

Fruit	Approx. volume or quantity	Weight in gms	Fruit	Approx. volume or quantity	Weight in gms
Apple	1 small	80	Ripe Mango	1/2	70
Banana	1/2 small	50	Orange	1	100
Watermelon	1 cup	175	Sweet lime	1	100
Fresh figs	2	50	Guava	1	100
Dried figs	2	30	Papaya	1 cup	80
Grapes	12	75	Pineapple	1 cup	80

(4) **Cereals :** When consumed in the specified quantities, the following cereals supply 15 gms of carbohydrates and 2 gms proteins (totally 68 calories) :

Jowar, bajra or wheat flour – $2\frac{1}{2}$ tablespoons (20 gms); khichri or boiled rice $\frac{1}{2}$ cup (100 gms); non-sweet biscuits (20 gms); boiled potatoes – 2 (100 gms); sweet potatoes – $\frac{1}{4}$ cup (50 gms).

(5) **Pulses :** Generally, 1 small container (katori or wati) of any cooked pulse supplies 125 to 140 calories.

(6) **Fats :** Approximate 45 calories are obtained from :
Butter, ghee or oil – 1 teaspoon (5 gms).
Cashewnuts, almonds, groundnuts – 10 gms.

(7) **Milk :** 1 cup of milk or curd supplies 12 gms of carbohydrates, 8 gms of proteins and 10 gms of fat (totally 170 calories). A reduction of 40 calories can be achieved by removing fat from the milk.

(8) **Non-vegetarian foods :** 30 gms of meat or fish or 1 (50 gm) egg supply 7 gm protein and 5 gm fats (totally 80 calories).

Given below is a model diet (1500–1600 calories) for the whole day, formulated on the basis of the above facts :

1. **Early morning :** 1 cup of non-sweetened milk, 1 cup of tea or coffee (with sachharine), 1 slice of bread or 2 puries or 2 khakras or 1 idli.

2. **Mid-morning :** 1 cup of buttermilk or some fruit.

3. **Lunch :** 2 small chapaties (with 1 teaspoon ghee), 1 cup of cooked vegetable, 1 cup of dal (cooked pulse), Salad of raw 'type A' vegetables, 1 cup of buttermilk or curd.

4. **Afternoon :** 1 cup tea or coffee (with sachharine), 2 slices of bread or 2–3 non-sweet biscuits.

5. **Dinner :** 1 cup of boiled rice or khichri (with 1 teaspoon ghee), 1 cup of dal or curry (flour-free), 1 cup of cooked vegetable, Salad of raw 'type A' vegetables, 1 cup butter milk or curd.

6. **Before retiring :** 3/4 to 1 cup of non-sweetened milk.

Notes : (1) Developing children, pregnant women or manual workers may need more food; obese persons should consume less food.

(2) Non-vegetarians can have an egg–omlette in the breakfast or meat (or fish) in a meal; but they should cut down the amount of other foods proportionately.

(3) Tables for food-substitution (which foods can be had instead of a particular food) have been given at the end of the book.

(4) Considering the fact that the size of chapaties or containers (katori or wati) is different in different homes, a diabetic should initially (for a few days) weigh his diet, to make certain that he does not exceed stipulated calories.

Sweetening agents to be used instead of sugar : Such sweetening agents include sachharine, fructose and sorbitol. Of these, sachharine is preferable since it has no nutritional value. It is about 350 times sweeter than sugar. It is available in the market in tablet or liquid forms. It should be noted that sachharine should not be added to food while cooking because extreme heat disintegrates it to create a very disagreeable and bitter taste. It should be added to foods after they have been cooked and while they are cooling.

Alcohol : Alcohol is a social menace. It variously harms the diabetic :

(1) It suddenly brings down the blood-sugar level, more so in those diabetics who take oral hypoglycemic drugs. A very low blood-sugar level may cause unconsciousness (hypoglycemic coma), a critical condition calling for urgent steps. Unfortunately, however, such unconscious persons get no attention because people think that he has collapsed due to excessive alcohol intake.

(2) It harms the liver.

(3) It stimulates the appetite and leads to obesity, whose connection with diabetes is well-known.

Some practical suggestions regarding diet :

(1) Diet control is extremely important and indispensable for diabetics. No drug can compensate for or undo the harm caused by faulty and reckless diet. Diet should be planned intelligently and on the basis of scientific principles. If due to false beliefs or misleading advices from relatives and neighbours, you are observing fasts or eating monotonous diet (e.g., chapaties and cooked karela) day after day, stop such practice immediately. A diet without variety not only arouses a feeling of dislike in the mind but also causes harm to the body. Always keep in the mind that for a diabetic, diet-control is not a temporary or passing phase but a life-long responsibility. Therefore give variety its due place in your diet. Use spices (in moderation though) because they possess no calorific value. Albeit, restrict the use of salt.

(2) Maintain the timings of your meals meticulously. If this is not done, it is well-nigh impossible to maintain the blood-sugar at normal levels all the time.

(3) However busy or occupied you may be, never miss a meal. This is necessary to prevent low blood-sugar.

(4) Be on your alert about correct and incorrect foods even when you go to hotels, parties or visit your relatives. Always keep sachharine tablets with you.

(5) While on a tour to some distant place, keep handy fruits like apple, orange or sweet lime. This will help in case symptoms of low blood sugar arise.

(6) Even if you do not have an appetite, do not abstain from food during an illness. Have light food of your liking at fixed timings.

(7) It is on the basis of the amount of your food in-take that your doctor has prescribed the dose of anti-diabetic drugs. Therefore do not vary the total amount of food you take during the day.

References :

1. Rosen, D. A., et al., Proc. Soc. Exp. Biol. Med. 88, 321, 1955
2. Wohl, M. G., et al., Proc. Soc. Exp. Biol. Med. 105, 523, 1960
3. Bersohn, I., et al., Lancet 1, 1020, 1957
4. Malkiel, S. B., et al., Med. Proc. 2, 455, 1956
5. Barnett, L. B., Clin. Physiol. 1, 26, 1959
6. Hjorth, P., Acta. Med. Scand. 105, 67, 1940
7. Bicknell, F., and Prescott, F., The vitamins in medicine, Lee Foundation for Nutritional Research, Milwaukee, Wis., 1953
8. Nut. Rev. 13, 325, 1955

9. Banerjee, S., et al., J. Biol. Chem. 190, 177, 1951
10. Murray, H. G., Proc. Soc. Exp. Biol. Med. 69, 351, 1948
11. Vogelsang, A., Ann. N. Y. Acad. Sci. 52, 397, 1949
12. Lee, P., Summary 8, 85, 1957
13. Kimble, M. S., et al., Am. J. Med Sci. 212, 574, 1946
14. Vorhaus, M. G., et al., Am. Med. Assn. 105, 1580, 1935
15. Henry A. Schroeder, The Trace Elements and Man, The Davin Adair Company, 1973

2. Exercises and Yoga

Physical exercise is the second important mode of treatment in diabetes.

Renowned Ayurvedic physician Maharshi Sushruta had advised diabetics to search for a cow lost in the forest. In other words he advised diabetics to flex their limbs. Today, however, forests are fast disappearing and cows are seldom lost. But there are several other ways of doing exercise.

Exercises yeild following benefits :

(1) Contracting muscles use up a lot of sugar. This relieves much of the pancreas' burden.

(2) Accumulated fat is used up. Consequently, weight decreases, which on itself may ameliorate most symptoms of diabetes.

(3) A psychological boost is experienced.

(4) Heart becomes more efficient.

A diabetic can opt for any light exercise like walking, jogging, swimming, cycling, gardening, etc. A middle-aged diabetic should desist from doing heavy or tiring exercises.

Before embarking upon the exercise programme the diabetic should go for a complete medical check up to ensure that no untoward incident occurs later on.

If during or after the exercise, execessive fatigue, breathlessness, weakness or chest-pain occurs, it is an indication that exercises have been overdone or that the amount or pace of the exercise is presently beyond the reach of the person.

Similarly, the diabetic should cut down the walking distance if he experiences sharp pain in calf muscles. He should take utmost care to prevent an injury to his body, especially his feet.

Even after commencing exercises, the food-intake should not be increased; otherwise benefits of exercise will be neutralised. A diabetic, who opts for exercise, should decrease the dose of oral antibiotic drugs or insulin as per his doctor's advice. It should be borne in mind that exercises reduce the amount of sugar in the blood. If a decrease in drugs commensurate with the severity of exercises is not brought about, the blood-glucose level may go below normal limits.

Regularity in exercises is of paramount importance. Exercises done irregularly may do more harm than good.

Yogasanas : Yogasanas (yogic postures) and pranayama (yogic breathing techniques) also have an important place in the treatment of diabetes. Several yoga experts and physicians, on numerous occasions, have proved the efficacy of yoga in bringing down the blood-sugar level.

Persons who cannot walk, jog or swim due to lack of desire (or unfavourable weather), persons who cannot undertake physical exercise because of a possibility of harming the kidneys or the heart and women who cannot spare special time for outdoor exercise can easily and safely obtain the benefits of exercise through yogasanas and pranayama. Even those persons who go for a walk or a swim in the morning can do yogasanas at some other time of the day when their stomachs are empty. Other forms of exercise and yoga can even be done on alternate days.

The following yogasanas have been proved to be beneficial to diabetics :

(1) Uddiyanbandh :

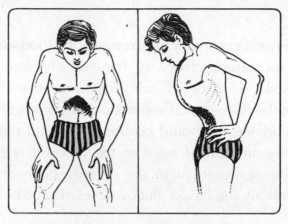

Fig. 7.2 : Uddiyanbandh

Stand keeping a distance of about 12 inches between the two feet. Stoop forward and place your palms on your thighs, slightly above the knee-caps. Exhale completely. Contract the abdominal muscles so as to pull the stomach backwards, toward the spine. This will elevate the diaphragm. Hold back the breath and remain in the above posture for a while. Then gradually release the abdominal muscles and inhale. Finally, straighten the body to attain the erect posture.

Initially, perform this asana twice. Thereafter gradually increase the number of repetitions to five.

(2) Yogamudra :

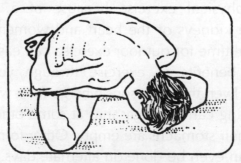

Fig. 7.3 : Yogamudra

Sit in the 'Padmasana (Lotus pose)', i.e., place the right foot on the left thigh and the left foot on the right thigh. Take both the arms behind the trunk and interlock the fingers. Now slowly bend the trunk forwards in an effort to touch the ground with the nose. Remain in this posture for a while. Finally straighten the body.

Initially perform this asana two times. Later, if time permits, step by step increase the number of repetitions to five.

(3) Trikonasana (the triangle pose) :

Fig. 7.4 : Trikonasana

Stand keeping a distance of 24 – 30 inches between the two feet. Keep the arms stretched at the sides. Now bend forwards (and slightly leftwards) and with the left hand try to touch the left big toe. At the same time, raise the right arm vertically upwards and look at its palm. Remain in this posture for a while. Then return to the erect position. Now perform the asana in the reverse direction, i.e., try to touch the right big toe with the right hand, elevate the left arm and look towards the left palm.

Initially perform this asana two times. As experience is gained with the passage of time, step by step increase the number of repetitions to five.

(4) Dhanurasana (the bow pose) :

Fig. 7.5 : Dhanurasana

Lie down prone on the ground. Bend the knees and with the hands, grasp the corresponding ankles. Now slowly raise the head, the chest and the legs. A beautiful arch will be formed. Hold back the breath. Remain in this posture for a while. Finally, exhaling bring the body back to the prone-lying position.

Repeat this asana two times.

(5) Pashchimottanasana (the back – stretching pose) :

Fig. 7.6 : Paschimottanasana

Sit on the ground with legs kept stretched forward. Now slowly bend the trunk forward and with the palms, try to touch (or hold) the corresponding toes. Also bend the head downwards in an effort to touch the knees with the nose. For the novices, this asana is difficult. But the final position can be achieved with practice. Hold the body in this posture for a while and then straighten the body.

Initially perform the asana twice. With the passage of time, step by step increase the number of repetitions to five.

(6) **Konasana :** This asana is considered a supplement to Pashchimottanasana.

Fig. 7.7 : Konasana

Sit on the ground with the legs stretched forward. Rest the palms on the ground, on either side of the body. Now straighten the arms, lock the elbow joints, move the feet forwards and raise the straight body. In this position the entire weight of the body will be borne by palms and soles. Bend the head backwards (i.e., downwards). Maintain this posture for a while. Finally revert back to the sitting position.

Initially, perform this asana two times. As experience is gained and if time permits, increase the number of repetitions, step by step, to five.

(7) **Sarvangasana** : Lie down supine on the ground. Slowly raise the straight legs upwards. Gradually raise the trunk too. Support the low back with the palms. Rest the elbows on the ground. Completely straighten the body and try to keep it vertical. After attaining the final pose, keep the body steady. Maintain this posture for about a minute. Finally, remove the palms from the back and gradually bring down the trunk and legs to the ground.

Fig. 7.8 : Sarvangasana

Initially perform this asana for a minute. Later, as experience is gained and if time permits, the asana can be prolonged, step by step, to five minutes.

(8) Matsyasana (the fish pose) :

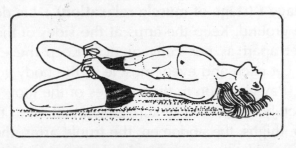

Fig. 7.9 : Matsyasana

Lie down supine on the ground. Place the left foot on the right thigh and right foot on the left thigh. With the palms, grasp the corresponding foot. Now slowly raise the trunk so as to form a hollow at the back. Bend the head backwards and rest it on the ground.

· Initially perform this asana for about 15 seconds. As experience is gained and if time permits, the duration can be increased, step by step, to two minutes.

(9) Shavasana (the corpse pose) : After performing the above mentioned eight asanas, Shavasana should be performed to rest the body completely.

No other posture can yield mental and physical rest in so short a time as Shavasana can. It is no wonder that Shavasana has been acclaimed as a sure remedy for mental tension and psychosomatic disorders, which abound in the present competitive and fast life.

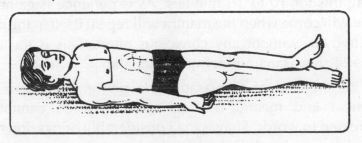

Fig. 7.10 : Shavasana

The asana can be divided into three stages :

Stage I (stage of muscle relaxation) : Lie down supine on the ground. Keep the arms at the sides of the body and the feet apart as per convenience. Keep the eyes closed. Relax. Let each and every muscle of the body go loose and flabby. Pay attention to the muscles of the foot. Relax them completely. Then turn by turn pay attention to the muscles of legs, thighs, the abdomen, the trunk, arms, the neck and the face and let them go completely. An onlooker should feel that there is no life in your body.

Stage II (stage of breath-control) : Now attend to the breathing process. Inhale slowly. Exhale slowly. Gradually slow down the pace of breathing as much as you can. An on-looker should feel that you are not breathing at all.

Stage III (stage of mind-control) : This is the most important stage of this asana. However, it is somewhat difficult and needs practice before it can be attained.

This stage aims at slowing down the thinking process and detaching the mind from worldly activities.

Concentrate on the breathing process. While inhaling chant 'so' in your mind. While exhaling chant 'ham' in your mind. Continue to concentrate on the breathing and to chant this mantra 'soham' in your mind. Initially the mind will waver and dwell in worldly matters. As soon as you realize this fact, engage the mind back to the mantra (japa). Continue doing this for 10 to 15 minutes. As experience is gained, a stage will come when the mantra will repeat itself in the mind on its own, without any conscious effort. This is the ideal stage of shavasana and termed 'Ajapajapa'.

At the end of Shavasana, the performer experiences physical and mental rest and peace which cannot be expressed in words. Shavasana considerably brings down the blood pressure and disburdens the heart.

Note : Scientists of the Jiwaji University at Gwalior have performed controlled experiments on 180 soldiers to determine the effects of pranayama (yogic breathing techniques) on diabetes. They made the soldiers perform two forms of pranayama : 'Ujjayi' and 'Bhasrika', 30 to 45 minutes a day for three months. The results of this experiment were most encouraging. The blood-sugar and blood-cholesterol levels of all the soldiers came down considerably. These results have been published in the 'Indian Journal of Medical Sciences'.

The procedures of Ujjayi pranayama and Bhasrika pranayama have been summarised below :

Ujjayi : Sit in the Padmasana pose. Keep the mouth shut. Fold the tongue inwards so that its lower surface comes in contact with the palate. Contract the uvula and the wall of the throat (including the glottis).

Now take a slow and very deep breath. Hold back the breath for as long as easily possible. Finally exhale slowly. Since the glottis remains half-closed, the breath while passing through it makes a peculiar sound.

During the entire process, one should feel that he is breathing through the throat and not through the nose.

With practice, the duration of Ujjayi can be gradually increased.

Bhasrika : Bhasrika is a Sanskrit word for bellows. This breathing technique is characterised by fast and forceful breaths, where the chest resembles bellows.

Sit in the Padmasana posture. Keep the mouth closed. Keep the body, neck and head erect. Breathe rapidly and forcefully ten times. Whilst breathing, contract and expand the lungs and the chest.

After the abovementioned ten rapid breaths, take a slow, deep breath. With the thumb and the index finger, clamp the nose and perform jalandhara bandh (i. e., bend the head forward and keep the chin pressed upon the uppermost part of the chest). Hold back the breath for as long as you easily can. Finally exhale slowly. This constitutes one round of Bhasrika.

After a short period of normal breathing repeat Bhasrika once more.

Initially limit the number of repetitions to three. With practice the frequency can be increased.

Special Note : When the blood-glucose concentration has soared to a very high level, it can be rapidly brought down with the help of a Hatha yoga practice called 'Shankha-prakshalana'.

This process should be performed early in the morning with an absolutely empty stomach. This process involves specific asanas. Hence the performer should wear loose clothes.

Procedure : Take a bucketful of slightly-salted warm water. Try to keep the mind calm. Rapidly drink two glasses of saline water from the bucket and perform the following asanas, eight times each.

(1) Tadasana :

Stand keeping a distance of 6 inches between the two feet. Interlocking the fingers raise both the arms above the head. Raise the heels from the ground, bend the head back and look at the palms. Stretch the body upwards as much as possible. Maintain the body in this posture for a while. Finally revert back to the starting position.

Repeat this asana eight times.

(2) Tiryaka Tadasana :

First assume the Tadasana pose.

Keeping the heels raised from the floor, first bend the trunk to the right and then to the left. The movement should mainly occur at the waist.

Repeat this asana eight times.

Fig. 7.11 : Tadasana

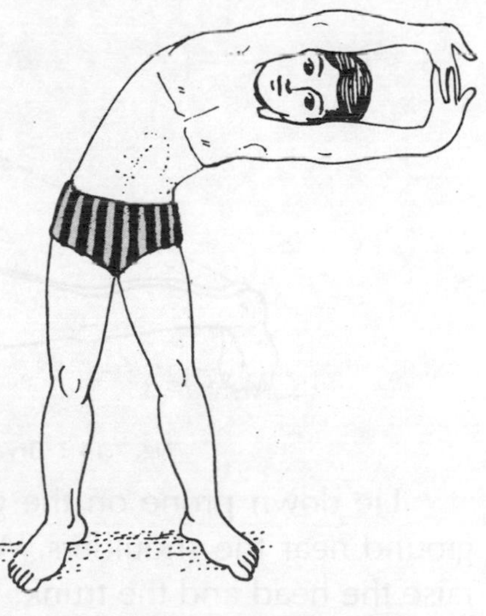

Fig. 7.12 : Tiryaka Tadasana

(3) Kati Chakrasana :

Stand keeping a distance of about 24 inches between the two feet. Keep the arms stretched at the sides, at level with the shoulders. Now turn the trunk towards the right, place the left palm on the right shoulder and take the right arm behind the back. Finally revert back to the starting position. Next time perform the asana in the reverse order.

Repeat the asana eight times on either side.

Fig. 7.13 : Kati
Chakrasana

(4) Tiryaka Bhujangasana :

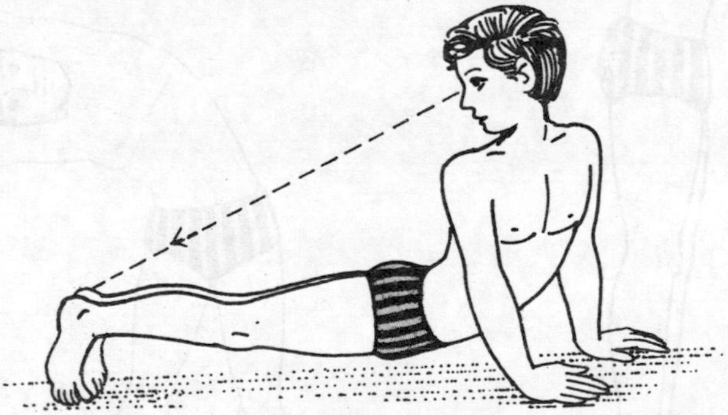

Fig. 7.14 : Tiryaka Bhujangasana

Lie down prone on the ground. Rest the palms on the ground near the shoulders. With the help of back muscles, raise the head and the trunk. Least weight should fall on the palms. Now turn the head and body to the right and look at the left heel. Then turn the head and the trunk to the left and look at the right heel. Finally revert back to the prone-lying position.

Repeat this asana eight times.

(5) Udaraakarshanasana :

Squat on the floor. Keep the palms on the knees. Now take the left knee downwards, turn the trunk to the right as much as possible and look backwards towards the right side. Revert back to the original position. Next perform the asana in the reverse direction.

Fig. 7.15 :
Udarakarshanasana

Repeat this asana eight times on either side.

When these five asanas are performed in the recommended order, alternate contraction and relaxation of some specific sphincter muscles of the digestive tract occur. Consequently the water drunk through the mouth rapidly moves downwards towards the anus, forcibly taking with it food and faeces.

Again drink two glasses of saline water and perform the five asanas, each eight times.

Now go to the toilet. Please do not use force to evacuate the bowels. Keep the abdominal muscles loose and relaxed. If stools are not passed within a minute, come out of the toilet.

Again drink two glasses of saline water, perform the five asanas, eight times each and go to the toilet. Never try to force out the stools.

Continue doing this, i.e., drinking 2 glasses of water, performing five asanas and going to the toilet.

Eventually stools will start coming out of the anus – initially solid and thereafter water-laden.

On continuing the whole process, finally a stage will come when only pure water passes out through the anus. This means that the whole digestive system has been emptied — a rare phenomenon. To attain this state, on an average 16 to 20 glasses of water are required.

Since this process is tiring, at the end of Shankha-prakshalana, a 45 to 60 minutes' rest is essential. For this, perform Shavasana.

During this period all the digestive organs and especially the pancreas and the liver get real rest and are consequently rejuvenised.

One hour after Shankha-prakshalana, the person should take a moderate meal of khichri. Papad, curry or chatni should not be eaten along with the khichri. On the following day, too, the person should eat a light diet, suitable for diabetics.

During the following days, the person should continue to perform 'Laghu Shankha-prakshalana'. In this method, the process of drinking two glasses of water and doing the five asanas is to be repeated only three times. Even this is sufficient to cause evacuation of the bowels.

Laghu Shankha-prakshalana should be performed every day for the first week and thereafter on alternate days during the second week. This regimen brings down the bloodsugar concentration drastically. Laghu Shankha-prakshalana can thereafter be performed once or twice a week.

It is desirable for persons suffering from complications of kidneys or the circulatory system, not to perform any variety of Shankha-prakshalana (or to perform it under an expert's guidance). It is also prohibited for all those persons for whom exercises are undesirable.

3. Medicines

[**Note :** In diabetes, an expert physician's services are invaluable and indispensable to determine the types of medicines and their dosage. In this respect, no article or book can ever take the place of the physician. The purpose of this chapter is only to provide a general overview of medicines used in diabetes.]

Two types of medicines are used in diabetes :
(1) Oral antidiabetic (hypoglycemic) drugs and
(2) Insulin, which is to be administered by an injection.

Oral hypoglycemic drugs : These drugs have been in use for last 30 – 35 years and are useful to almost half of all diabetics. They have no resemblance whatsoever to insulin. Oral hypoglycemic drugs are of two types : (1) Sulphonylurea group of drugs and (2) Biguanides.

Sulphonylurea drugs stimulate the beta cells of the pancreas to produce more insulin. Besides they also prevent glucose present in the liver from entering the blood stream.

Biguanides increase the utilisation (though unnaturally) of glucose present in the blood by peripheral muscles.

In short, both these drugs strive to decrease the blood – glucose concentrations.

More details about these drugs have been given in the table below :

No.		Sulphonylurea Drugs					Phenethyl Biguanide
		First Generation		Second Generation			
		Tolbutamide	Chlorpropamide	Glybenclamide	Glypizide	Glyclazide	Phenformin
1	Dose	500 to 2000 mg	250 to 500 mg	2.5 to 20 mg	5 to 20 mg	80 to 300 mg	40 to 50 mg
2	Hypoglycemic effect	Potent	Very potent	Very potent	Very potent	Very potent	Moderate
3	Absorption through intestine	In 30 minutes	In 1 hour	Very fast	Very fast	Very fast	After 1 hour
4	Excretion through the body	After 6 hours	After 35–40 hours	After 12–24 hours	After 10–16 hours	After 10–20 hours	After 6–12 hour
5	Side effects	Rare	In 8% patients	In 5% patients	Rare	Rare	In many patients
6	Mode of action	Stimulate the beta cells of the pancreas; inhibit the liver from liberating glucose into the blood-stream					Increase the peripheral utilisation of glucose; Hamper the production of glucose by the liver.
7	Effective in	Maturity onset (NID) diabetes; Useless in juvenile diabetes, ketosis, unconsciousness & infections					Maturity onset diabetes; sometimes also useful in juvenile diabetes
8	Long term effectiveness	Effectiveness may wane after prolonged use; however, one drug may be replaced by another to obtain the desired results					Effective even after prolonged use

> **Note :** From amongst the sulphonylurea drugs. Tolbutamide (Rastinon) is probably the best and the mildest. It is a general practice to prescribe 1 gm of this drug in the morning and 0.5 gm in the evening.
>
> Chlorpropamide (Diabinese) is also commonly used for diabetes A 250 mg dose of this drug once a day (in the morning) is considered adequate.
>
> Second generation sulphonylurea drugs like Glybenclamide, Glypizide, Glyclazide are also becoming popular in our country. The advantage of these drugs is that they are effective in very small doses.

Side-effects of oral drugs include hypoglycemia, nausea vomitting, diarrhoea, liver disorders, jaundice, blood disorders and ketosis.

Oral hypoglycemic drugs are indicated in :

(1) Stable and maturity onset type of diabetes of recent onset which cannot be controlled on diet alone.

(2) Where the insulin requirement is upto 40 units.

(3) Diabetics who are not ketotic, i.e., whose blood has not been poisoned by the products of incomplete metabolism of fats.

(4) Diabetics with visual, neurological or psychic defects who cannot take insulin injections by themselves.

Oral hypoglycemic drugs are useless in :

(1) Unstable and thin diabetics

(2) Juvenile diabetics

(3) Diabetics who are prone to ketoacidosis

(4) Acute complications of diabetes

(5) Surgery

(6) Pregnancy

(7) Febrile (body-temperature raising) infections

(8) Physically stressful conditions like a heart attack, cerebral haemorrhage, etc.

Insulin : Diabetes is a disease which arises due to a relative or absolute deficiency of insulin. 'Diabetics should be benefitted by giving them insulin from outside', so thought scientists and rightly so. Vigorous attempts to procure insulin from animals followed. Finally in 1921 A. D., Banting and Best succeeded in isolating pure insulin from the extract of animal pancreas. For this contribution to the treatment of diabetes, the names of Banting and Best shall be written in letters of gold.

Insulin revolutionised the treatment of diabetes. It robbed the disease of its fatality. At one time almost all child diabetics and many adult diabetics succumbed to diabetic coma. Insulin has provided a fresh lease of life to such diabetics. In the treatment of diabetes, the place of insulin is unique.

Like the insulin produced in a person's body, externally given insulin too brings down the level of blood–glucose.

To whom and when is insulin useful or essential?

(1) Insulin should be used without delay in acute ketoacidosis and diabetic coma.

(2) For all juvenile diabetics, who cannot manufacture insulin in their own bodies, external insulin is a must.

(3) Insulin is essential for lean diabetics.

(4) For pregnant diabetic women, insulin is indispensable. They cannot be given oral antidiabetic drugs.

(5) Insulin is essential for those diabetics who have contracted febrile infections.

(6) Insulin is essential for persons suffering from complications of diabetes.

(7) Insulin is indispensable for the control of diabetes prior to or during a surgery on the diabetic.

(8) Insulin is indispensable in pancreatic diabetes.

(9) Insulin is useful to those women in whom itching on and around the genitals cannot be cured by any other measure.

Types of insulin : Types of medicinal insulin and their characteristics have been tabulated below :

Type	Appearance	Onset of effects	Maximum effectiveness	Total duration of effectiveness
(A) Insulins with rapid but short-term effects				
1. Crystalline	Transparent	In about half an hour	After 3 – 4 hours	5 to 8 hours
2. Isoinsulin	Transparent	Within one hour	After 3 – 4 hours	12 to 14 hours
3. Semilente	Milky	Within one hour	After 3 – 4 hours	12 to 14 hours
4. Actrapid	Transparent	In about 15 minutes	After 3 – 4 hours	8 to 12 hours
(B) Insulins with intermediate effects				
1. Globin	Transparent	Within one hour	After 8 – 10 hours	18 to 20 hours
2. N. P. H.	Milky	Within two hours	After 8 – 10 hours	24 to 30 hours
3. Lente	Milky	Within two hours	After 8 – 10 hours	24 to 30 hours
4. Rapitarl	Transparent	Within three hours	After 8 – 10 hours	18 to 20 hours
(C) Insulins with slow but long-term effects				
1. Protamine zinc	Milky	In 4 to 8 hours	After 12 to 24 hours	upto 36 hours
2. Ultralente	Milky	In 6 to 8 hours	After 16 to 24 hours	upto 36 hours

Lente and N. P. H. insulins are much more commonly used and popular than other varieties of insulin. Generally a single injection of Lente insulin everyday is sufficient to control the blood-sugar of almost 60 – 70 per cent of diabetics. This injection is to be administered by the patient himself, 20 – 30 minutes before the morning breakfast.

Previously, the tradition of mixing a short acting (e.g., crystalline) with an intermediate acting (e.g., N. P. H.) insulin was in vogue. But with the invention of Lente insulin, this practice is rapidly waning.

Rapidly acting varieties of insulin are presently used mainly in emergency conditions (e.g., diabetic coma), where the well-being or life of the patient is at stake.

Monocomponent Insulin : Commonly used insulins possess impurities like proinsulin, desamido insulin, glucagon, pancreatic polypeptide and somatostatin in minute amounts. By chromatographic purification techniques, scientists have succeeded in getting rid of such impurities and manufacturing extremely pure 'monocomponent insulin'. Such pure insulin is naturally very effective.

Uses of monocomponent insulin :

(1) When common insulin gives rise to an allergic reaction.

(2) When insulin is required only for short durations (e.g., during pregnancy or surgery).

(3) When due to resistance developed inside the body, the requirement of common insulin exceeds 100 units per day.

(4) When commonly used insulin gives rise to destruction of fat-cells beneath the skin (lipodystrophy).

Semisynthetic human-insulin : In 1978, scientists succeeded in manufacting semisynthetic human-insulin by 'recombinant D. N. A. technique'. In this method, the human gene responsible for the manufacture of insulin are tran-planted into the bodies of bacteria called 'E Coli'. Thereafter, these bacteria start manufacturing an insulin which is fast-acting and exactly similar to human-insulin. Such insulin can be used for very strict vegetarians too. This 'human-insulin', however, has been observed to excite a response of resistance or allergy in certain patients.

At present, such human-insulin is available in Denmark and other western countries.

The dosage of insulin : The task of determining the ideal dosage of insulin for a particular patient is very complicated and should be left alone to the physician. An ideal dosage of insulin is the one which continuously maintains the blood sugar level within normal limits. Some patients require as low a dose as 10 – 12 units per day. Others require 100 units or even more insulin every day. On an average 30 to 40 units of insulin, has been found an effective dose.

To a diabetic, who has no other complication, most doctors usually first give 20 units of Lente insulin per day. Three to four days after commencing the treatment, urine samples, obtained during the course of the day, are analysed for sugar. Depending upon the absence or presence of sugar in the urine, the insulin dosage is decreased or increased, respectively.

Once the ideal dose of insulin has been determined, the patient should follow that dosage faithfully and should make no changes in the dosage on his own.

Factors that can necessitate a change in the insulin dosage :

Factors that increase insulin-requirements	Factors that decrease insulin-requirements
• An increase in the weight of the body	• A decrease in body-weight
• An increased intake of food	• Less than normal food – intake
• A decrease in physical exertion	• Unaccustomed physical exertion
• Pregnancy	• Post-pregnancy period
• Intake of thyroid, epinephrine or corticoid drugs	• After the drugs indicated on LHS have been stopped
• An acute infectious disease	• Complete control of the infection
• Fever	• After fever has come down
• Ketosis	• After ketosis has been cured

If one of the above conditions arises, a change in the insulin dosage is required. However, the degree of the essential change can be determined only by a physician.

Method of taking insulin injection : It is not only desirable but extremely essential that every diabetic learns to inject insulin in his body himself. A person who solely relies upon his doctor (or a member of his family) for insulin injections may find himself in difficulty if he or his physician is on a tour. In fact, injecting insulin on one's self is an extremely simple procedure.

Material needed :

(1) **Syringe :** 2 c.c. syringe, preferably of glass. Each c.c. must be divided into 10 parts. 1/10 c.c. = 4 units if 1 c.c. insulin contains 40 units. 1/10 c.c. = 8 units if 1 c.c. insulin contains 80 units.

(2) **Needles :** A long and stout needle to draw insulin from the bottle. A small (1.25 cms) and thin (no. 25 or 26) needle for insertion into the body.

(3) **Spirit (or some other antiseptic) :** To cleanse the skin and the cap of the insulin-bottle.

(4) **Clean cotton**

(5) **Insulin bottle :** The strength of the insulin should first be ascertained from the label to avoid difficulty. In the market, insulin is available in varying strengths, mainly 40 units/c.c. and 80 units/c.c.

(6) **Forceps :** To lift the syringe or the needle lying in boiling water (it is necessary to sterilise the syringe and the needle by boiling them prior to their use). It is a general practice to keep the used needles or syringes immersed in alcohol.

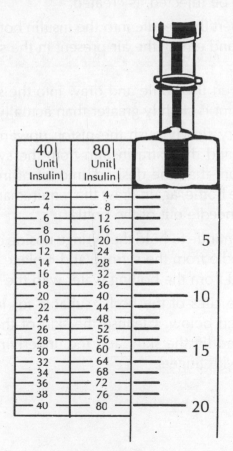

40| Unit| Insulin|	80| Unit| Insulin|	
2	4	
4	8	
6	12	
8	16	
10	20	5
12	24	
14	28	
16	32	
18	36	
20	40	10
22	44	
24	48	
26	52	
28	56	
30	60	15
32	64	
34	68	
36	72	
38	76	
40	80	20

Fig. 7.16

Steps to effect an injection :

(1) First of all, roll the insulin vial (bottle) between the palms for a minute or two to render the contents homogeneous.

(2) Clean the rubber-cap of the bottle with spirit.

(3) Lift the syringe out of the boiling water, with the forceps. Transfer the syringe to the left hand. Lift the long needle out of the boiling water and fix it to the syringe.

(4) Draw the piston out of the syringe to such an extent that an air-filled space, whose volume is equal to the amount of insulin to be injected, is created.

(5) Insert the needle into the insulin bottle through the rubber cap and empty the air present in the syringe into the bottle.

(6) Invert the bottle and draw into the syringe, insulin whose amount is slightly greater than actually required.

(7) Very slowly push the piston upwards to drive out air bubbles and the extra insulin from the syringe. If while doing so more than the desired amount of insulin is driven back into the bottle, again draw the required amount. Finally, remove the needle out of the bottle.

(8) Continue to hôld the syringe upside down. Remove the long needle from the syringe and replace it by the small needle, lifted from the boiling water with the forceps.

(9) The sites of the body, suitable for injections have been depicted below. Cleanse the skin of the selected site with spirit and lift the skin (and the underlying muscles) by pinching it with fingers.

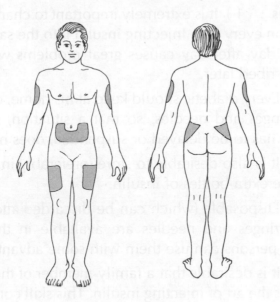

Fig. 7.17 : Sites where insulin can be safely injected

(10) Steadily and firmly insert the needle beneath the skin, almost vertically downwards, till about 2/3 of the needle has penetrated inside the body.

(11) Press the piston to completely release the insulin into the body.

(12) Finally withdraw the needle from the body and gently massage the punctured part of the skin with cotton soaked in spirit.

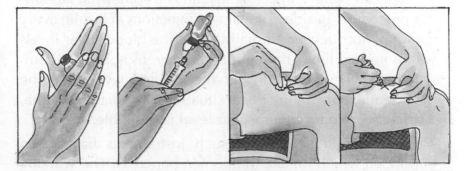

Fig. 7.18 : Steps in insulin injection

Notes : (1) It is extremely important to change the site of injection every day. Injecting insulin into the same part of the body day after day causes great problems which have been described later.

(2) Every diabetic should keep at his home, one or two extra syringes and needles, so that a situation, where the treatment has to be delayed or suspended, does not arise.

(3) It is also desirable to store (preferably in a refrigerator) some extra bottles of insulin.

(4) Disposable (which can be discarded after a single usage) syringes and needles are available in the market. Affording persons can use them with some advantage.

(5) It is desirable that a family-member of the diabetic, too, learns the art of injecting insulin. This skill comes handy when the diabetic is unconscious or incapacitated by some illness.

(6) For those diabetics who fear the needle excessively, needleless syringes or guns are available in big cities. After filling such a gun with the required amount of insulin, a high pressure is built up inside. The gun is then held in contact of diabetic's skin and the trigger of the gun released. Insulin released with great force and speed, pierces the skin and enters the body.

Special Note : Injecting insulin is a somewhat labourious procedure. Besides, one or two injections of insulin every day may not succeed in maintaining the blood-sugar levels within normal limits throughout the day. In normal circumstances, slight fluctuations of blood-sugar levels may be inconsequential. But in critical situations, like diabetic coma, a stricter control of blood-sugar level is desirable.

To serve this purpose, such instruments have been developed which imitate the human pancreas. The working of a large instrument, commonly used in hospitals, is quite simple. A tube (of the machine) continuously draws blood from the patient's body and sends it to the instrument, where the blood is continuously analysed for its glucose-content. Then as per the requirements, either insulin or glucagon is released into the patient's body. This instrument is, however, too large and cumbersome. It cannot be used outside the hospital or cannot keep the patient ambulent. In fact, at present it is used only to tide over a critical phase, i.e., for a day or two.

Efforts have also been made to develop much smaller instruments that a diabetic can wear on his body and continue his day to day activities. One such instrument, available in western countries, needs to be worn on the waist belt. The needle of this instrument remains pierced into the patient's body. This instrument has no glucose-sensor to analyse blood-glucose level. Some insulin continuously enters the patient's body. After a snack or a meal, the patient has to compress an elastic pump present on the instrument, to release additional quota of insulin, commensurate to the need.

The idea of developing an instrument which could be transplanted beneath the skin and which would work exactly like human pancreas is being actively pursued.

A diagrammatic model of this instrument has been presented below :

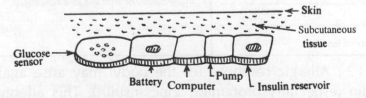

Fig. 7.19 : Transplanted artificial pancreas

The sensor present in this gadget will continuously evaluate the glucose level of the blood. Thereafter insulin from the glucose reservoir of the gadget will be continuously released into the body as per the need. Such gadget is likely to be available in the near future.

Side-effects of insulin :

(1) Unconsciousness may occur due to blood-glucose level falling much below the physiological limit (i.e., 50 mg %). Such unconsciousness is termed 'hypoglycemic coma'.

The symptoms that precede unconsciousness include excessive fatigue and weakness, hunger, headache, giddiness, cold sweating, etc. If not treated immediately, the patient falls unconscious.

Such a situation may arise in a diabetic's life any time. It is precisely for this reason that every diabetic should always keep in his pocket a card, as depicted below :

Name	**I HAVE DIABETES**
Address	If I am found behaving strangely or
....	unconscious, I may be suffering from low
....	blood-sugar.
Phone	If I am able to swallow, give me a sweet
Doctors' Name	drink or a fruit-Juice. Wait for 10–15
Address	minutes.
....	If I am unconscious, call my doctor
Phone	immediately or shift me to a hospital.
I take	
variety of insulin.	

(2) Allergic response (of the body) may arise against insulin (especially protamine zinc insulin). This allergy is manifested by red coloured rashes on the skin or swelling.

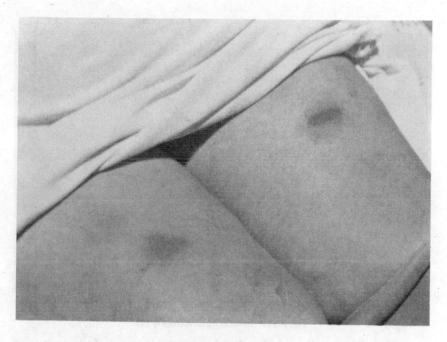

Fig. 7.20 : Insulin allergy

(3) About 25 to 35 per cent of child diabetics suffer from lipodystrophy, i.e., fat cells beneath the skin at the site of injections may get destroyed. This gives an extremely unsightly and grotesque appearance to the skin.

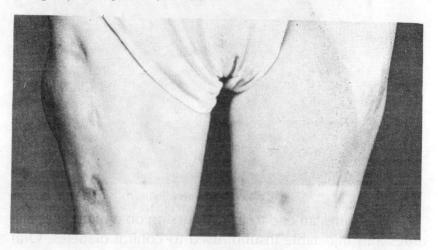

Fig. 7.21 : Insulin lipodystrophy (1)

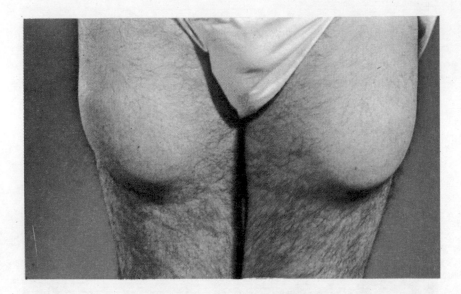

Fig. 7.21 : Insulin lipodystrophy (2)

(4) The cells of the body at and around the site of insulin injections may die and rot (insulin necrosis).

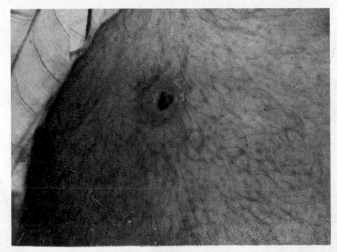

Fig. 7.22 : Insulin necrosis

This brings an end to the discussion on oral antidiabetic drugs and injectable insulin, used to control diabetes. Oral drugs and insulin can be used independently or in conjunction.

Ayurveda, too, has recommended many a drug or herb to combat diabetes. These include leaves of madhnashi (gudmar), roots of tondli (tindora) and sadaphuli, extracts of onion and garlic, concoction of neem leaves, karela juice, powdered jamun seeds, shilajit and jasad bhasma. Of these, karela juice, shilajit, jasad bhasma and powdered jamun seeds have been seen to have a slight beneficial effect in some cases. It should, however, be noted that jamun fruits are rich (15%) in sugar and are prohibited for diabetics.

Homoeopathy recommends Acid phosphoric, Metallic silver and Sulphate of soda for diabetes. But all these drugs have proved worthless in controlled clinical trials.

In fact, after the invention of powerful sulphonylurea and biguanide drugs, all indigenous and homoeopathic drugs are fast waning from the limelight.

4. Acupuncture or Acupressure

Acupuncture and Acupressure are oriental therapies which utilise certain points on the surface of the body to influence internal organs. In Acupuncture, specific points are pierced with needles whereas in Acupressure, the same points are stimulated by deep pressure with a finger-tip or a blunt object. The W. H. O. has given due recognition to these therapies.

It has been seen time and again that when acupuncture or acupressure treatment is added to diet and exercise, the need of medicines diminishes considerably. In quite a few cases, medicines can be discarded altogether.

Diabetes is a life-long disease and its control a life-time responsibility. In diabetes, acupressure is preferable to acupuncture because the former can be performed by the patient himself.

The following Acupressure points have proved effective in bringing down the blood sugar level :

Fig. 7.23

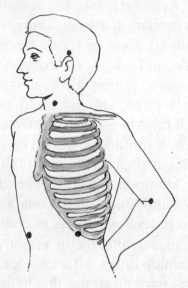

Fig. 7.24

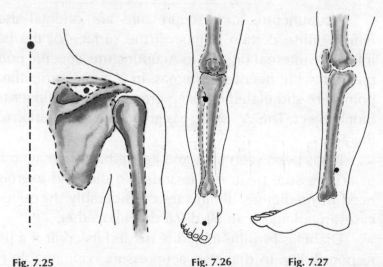

Fig. 7.25   Fig. 7.26   Fig. 7.27

The description of acupressure points :

(1) Point located on the middle of an imaginary vertical line, joining the anteriorly folded ears.

(2) Point located on the side of the forehead, exactly above the vertex of the anteriorly folded ear.

(3) Point located on the side of the neck, four finger-breadths lateral to the adam's apple.

(4) Point located at the outer end of the crease formed by completely flexing the elbow.

(5) Point located at the front end of the penultimate rib.

(6) Point located at the back of the neck, below the most prominently seen vertebra, when the head is bent forward.

(7) Point located at the back of the shoulder.

(8) Point located four finger-breadths below the lower border of the round knee bone and one finger-breadth lateral to the verticle midline, after the knee has been bent at a right angle.

(9) Point located in the fleshy part between the first and the second toes.

(10) Point located four finger-breadths above the inner prominence of ankle bone, slightly towards the posterior side.

Method of giving pressure : Each point should be rythmically pressed for a minute, with the finger (or thumb) tip or the blunt end of a pencil. Treatment can be had at any time, but the time $2\frac{1}{2}$ hours after meals is preferable.

Acupressure treatment is absolutely safe and devoid of side-effects. Yet it is considerably effective as can be seen from successful clinical trials and the statistical data available.

5. Magnet Therapy

Among new modes of treatment, Magnet therapy occupies a very important place. Numerous evidences are pouring in from several research centres showing that Magnet therapy is highly effective in the treatment of many diseases.

Diabetes can be controlled and its complications (e.g., atherosclerosis, high blood pressure and coronary artery disease) can be effectively prevented by Magnet therapy. Numerous proofs are available to validate the above claim.

The pancreas gland can be stimulated by placing two moderately strong magnets on the back, slightly above the imaginary horizontal line passing through the navel. The magnets thus act like sulphonylurea drugs, i.e., they increase the secretion of insulin. Therefore Magnet therapy is particularly indicated in the adult variety of diabetes.

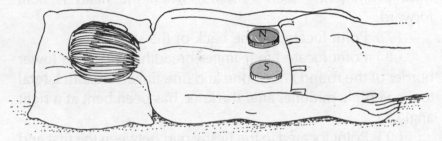

Fig. 7.28 : Magnet therapy in diabetes

Water, placed in a strong magnetic field for about 24 hours, gets magnetised. Such magnetised water, drunk 3-4 times a day (a cupful every time) also helps the diabetic. Magnetised water beneficially affects the digestive, the circulatory and the urinary systems.

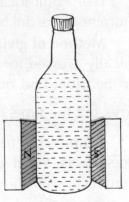

Fig. 7.29 : Magnetising water

The science of Magnet therapy is still in its infancy. Yet proofs about its effectiveness are pouring in. Numerous laboratories around the world are working incessantly to determine the efficacy of Magnet therapy.

It is not only desirable but very essential that Magnet therapy be also employed, along with other measures, to prevent or to control diabetes.

Chapter in a nutshell :

1. The treatment of diabetes should be continued throughout the life.

2. In the treatment of diabetes, the patient has to shoulder a greater responsibility than the physician.

3. The chief goal of diabetic treatment is to maintain the blood-sugar level in the normal range round the clock.

4. Diet is the single most important factor in the treatment of diabetes. Without correct dietray changes, diabetes cannot be successfully dealt with.

5. It was once believed that carbohydrate–containing foods should be excluded from a diabetic's diet. However, this view finds no favour with the present-day physicians.

6. A diabetic should consume a balanced diet which possesses all the constituents necessary for the body, e.g., carbohydrates (60%), fats (22%), proteins (18%), vitamins, minerals and fibres.

7. A diabetic should refrain from eating foods that contain refined sugar. Sachharine should be used in the place of sugar to sweeten milk, tea or coffee.

8. A diabetic should never overeat. Instead of taking two heavy meals a day, he should consume the same amount of food in three to four equally divided parts.

9. In the treatment of diabetes, the importance of exercise is second only to that of diet.

10. The muscles, due to their contractions during an exercise, use up a lot of sugar from the blood. This disburdens the pancreas.

11. A diabetic should perform light exercises like walking, jogging, swimming or cycling. He should also perform yogasanas.

12. Before embarking upon the exercise programme, a diabetic should undergo a complete medical check-up (especially that for the heart and the kidneys) as a safeguard against an untoward incident in the future.

13. If diabetes is not adequately controlled with diet and exercise, the patient should start medical treatment as per his physician's advice.

14. Two types of medicines are used in the treatment of diabetes : insulin and oral hypoglycemic agents.

15. Insulin is not usually required in maturity onset diabetes. Oral antidiabetic drugs suffice.

16. Insulin is inevitable for juvenile diabetics (or those adult diabetics whose disease is not controlled by oral drugs alone).

17. Every diabetic (and his near ones too) should learn the art of administering an insulin injection to one's self.

18. After the invasion of modern (sulphonylurea) drugs, Ayurvedic and Homoeopathic medicines for diabetes have faded away from the limelight.

19. Acupressure and Magnet therapy should also be employed in the treatment of diabetes. These therapies help in minimising the dosage of medicines, thereby cutting down the risk of side-effects.

8. PREVENTION OF DIABETES

The old adage 'Prevention is better than cure' is especially true for diabetes.

(1) It is desirable that a man with diabetes (or with a possibility of developing diabetes) does not marry a woman with diabetes (or with a possibility of developing diabetes). If both the parents are diabetics, their children almost certainly inherit the disease.

Before giving consent for the marriage, it is becoming customary these days to match the horoscopes of the prospective bride and the groom, to ascertain that their stars are favourable to each other. In fact, it is more essential to know whether either of them has a family history of diabetes (or other inheritable diseases). It is also desirable to know the blood-group of the other person.

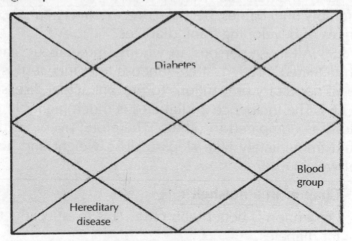

(2) Incorrect dietary habits play a major role in the development of diabetes. Parents should take great care to form correct dietary habits in their children. Children should be prevented from becoming addicts of icecream, cakes, jam, jelly, peppermint, chocolates and other sweets. The amount of food given to children should be such as would allow growth but not obesity. Ideal (or less than ideal) weight and a proportionate (or silm) body is an almost certain guarantee against diabetes.

Person with a family history of diabetes should accept voluntary diet-control after the age of 30 years, since physical development has been completed. This is inevitable for sedentary and obese persons.

(3) Every person should include in his or her daily-schedule, regular physical exercise and yoga. Parents should convince their children about the paramount importance of exercise and should encourage them for outdoor sports.

(4) Mothers who give birth to very large and heavy babies may be in a pre-diabetic stage. They should be all the more conscious about their diet, lest dormant diabetes should get converted into established diabetes. It is also desirable that such mothers do not give birth to more than two (preferably one) babies, because every delivery enhances the chances of developing frank diabetes.

(5) All those persons, in whom a prediabetic state has been detected through 'stress glucose tolerance test', should take all necessary precautions to prevent actual disease.

(6) The incidence of diabetes is much higher in obese persons as compared to others. Therefore, every fat person should immediately take steps to lose weight and achieve ideal weight.

Chapter in a nutshell :

1. Prevention is better than cure. This is especially true for diabetes.
2. Persons having a family history of diabetes should not intermarry.
3. Persons desirous of preventing diabetes should culti- vate proper dietary habits, should eat moderately and refrain from consuming too many sweet foods. Unless obesity is prevented, diabetes cannot be kept off for long.
4. Regular exercise plays an important role in preventing diabetes.

9. SKIN AND FOOT-CARE

In diabetes, care of the skin and the feet assumes paramount importance. Increased chances of contracting an infection, inadequate blood-supply and impaired sensations are the three factors which endanger a diabetic's skin and feet.

Skin-care : A diabetic should always remain alert to prevent an injury to the skin. He should take extra care while scratching his skin or while shaving. He should see that his skin is not abrased against the wall or a rough surface.

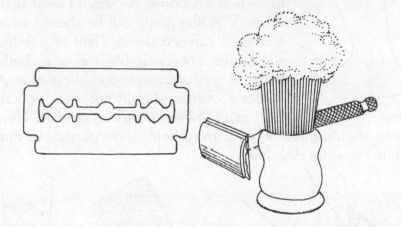

In spite of all the precautions, if the skin is injured, the wound should not be allowed to get infected. It should be washed with clean water, disinfected with a cotton-swab soaked in alcohol and lightly bandaged with a cotton cloth. Adhesive tapes should never be used to cover a wound. If a need is felt, mild antiseptics like mercurochrome, acriflavine or furazolidine can be applied over the wound; but strong medicines like tincture of iodine, carbolic acid, salicylic acid or phenol should be avoided.

Foot-care : 'Care for your feet more than your face', so advise the doctors to their diabetic patients, and rightly so.

A diabetic should constantly be on an alert to prevent a foot-injury.

The feet should be washed twice a day with soap and warm water. While washing the feet, the nails, the toes and the skin between the toes should be minutely observed. The feet should then be wiped dry with a soft cloth. In diabetics, the skin between the toes easily gets injured or infected with fungus. So a diabetic, after washing his feet, should apply a cream or an ointment like lanolin between his toes.

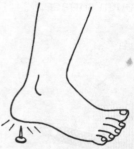

A diabetic should never move barefooted. In his home, he should wear light slippers. While going out he should wear soft (e.g., canvas) shoes. Tight or pointed shoes are not desirable for a diabetic because they obstruct blood-circulation. A diabetic woman should not wear pencil-heel or high-heel shoes or sandals. New shoes should initially be worn only for short periods so that a bite does not develop.

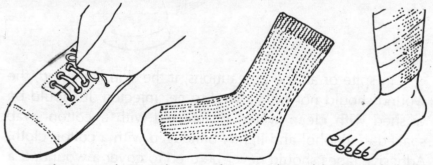

Elastic, nylon socks are also not desirable for a diabetic as they impede blood-circulation. Instead, cotton socks should be worn. A diabetic should also desist from using bandages over his calves or knees (knee-caps) or from wearing an underwear that is tight around the thighs. A diabetic should not sit cross-legged (with one knee lying above the other) for long periods because this obliterates the popliteal artery lying at the back of the knee and jeopardizes the blood circulation of the leg.

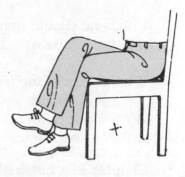

A diabetic should cut his nails with great care. It is desirable to cut the nails when they are soft after a bath or after immersing the feet in warm water for some time. The nails should not be excessively trimmed.

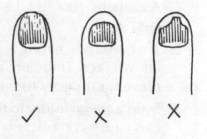

A diabetic should never cut corns on his soles himself. Such tasks should be left to the physician. Hot water bottles or bags should not be used to alleviate pain or numbness in the legs.

It is very essential for a diabetic to spend about ten minutes every day keeping the entire legs elevated and doing foot and ankle exercises as depicted below :

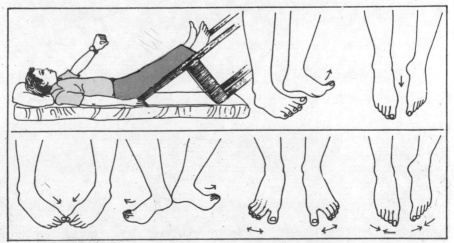

Exercises to maintain foot-health

A diabetic should immediately consult his doctor, if :

(1) there is pain, itching, swelling or numbness of the legs,

(2) the skin of the leg suddenly changes colour,

(3) a leg-wound gets infected and an ulcer is formed,

(4) a foot-disorder does not improve with home remedies, within a short time.

Chapter in a nutshell :

1. A diabetic should take extra care of his skin and his feet.

2. That wound-healing is delayed in diabetics is a well known fact. Therefore a diabetic should take care to prevent an injury to the skin.

3. Even a trivial injury to the foot or a toe of the diabetic can cause complications or even gangrene. Hence a diabetic should always be on the alert to prevent an injury to his feet.

4. A diabetic should keep his entire legs elevated for 5 – 10 minutes every day and move his toes and feet. This ensures the health of the feet.

10. LIFE WITH DIABETES

The diagnosis of diabetes evokes different responses in different persons.

That a child diabetic cannot understand the gravity of the diagnosis can readily be understood. But many a time, even adults react childishly. Many patients just refuse to accept the situation. This refusal is expressed in different forms. Some patients bluntly state that they can't have diabetes. Some others, who look at the diagnosis with suspicion, go from one physician to another and request for repeat laboratory investigations, as if in search of a physician who would favour them by saying, 'You do not have diabetes.' Even after being presented with irrefutable proofs and made to accept the bitter truth, such patients take medicines irregularly or in lesser doses. To some patients, the diagnosis diabetes gives a great jolt or a shock. Unending worry then overpowers them. Some patients do accept the diagnosis, but they hide it from their near and dear ones.

However, as time passes, most diabetics come out of the shock, assume a more mature behaviour and sincerely start following their physician's advice.

In fact, there is no need at all for a diabetic to be unduly upset or feel ashamed. Millions of people in this world have diabetes. A patient who has reshaped his mind and is determined, can launch an assault against the disease. Today diabetics can boast of an almost normal and creative long life. Diabetics no longer die of acute complications like diabetic coma or gangrene. Diabetic pregnant women give birth to healthy babies at the right time. Life insurance corporations have started accepting insurance proposals from diabetics. These facts are indications of the progress made in the understanding and the treatment of the disease.

The life-picture of diabetes has undergone a complete change during the past 75 years. The statistical data given below is a testimony to this fact.

No.	Factor	1915 A.D.	1987 A.D.
1	Average longevity of life after onset of diabetes in adults	4.7 years	20 years
2	Average longevity of life after onset of diabetes in children	1 to 2 years	27 years
3	Average age at the time of death	44.5 years	64.7 years
4	Incidence of diabetic coma	64.0%	1.0%
5	Incidence of death during surgery	7.3%	3.3%

Diabetes is not a blow that has been struck by fate in retaliation of sins committed in the previous birth. A person should not think that diabetes is a 'fruit of karma' and that one can do nothing but meekly suffer it. The fact is that diabetes is a disease determind by heredity and precipitated by incorrect life-style, especially faulty dietary habits. With intelligent steps, the disease can be controlled and the life-span lengthened.

After the diagnosis of the disease, the diabetic (and his family members too) should strive to gather information regarding each and every aspect of this disease. If knowledge about (1) principles of dieting and exercise, (2) the dosage of insulin and the method of injecting it, (3) symptoms and treatment of low blood-sugar (hypoglycemia), (4) causes, symptoms and treatment of diabetic coma and (5) skin and foot care is acquired, a diabetic can lead a happy, fruitful and long life.

Equipped with complete knowledge about the disease and with the support of the physician, the diabetic should launch an assault against the disease, first with non-medicinal weapons like diet, exercise, Acupressure and Magnet therapy. After commencing the treatment, he should get his urine and blood examined to assess the degree of control achieved.

It should be clearly understood that mere amelioration of symptoms is not a proof of the control of diabetes. For that, a periodic analysis of urine and blood is inevitable.

Diabetes can be said to be under control only when :

(1) Symptoms of diabetes are absent,

(2) Patient's ideal body-weight is maintained,

(3) Blood sugar levels are within the normal range,

(4) Sugar does not escape in the urine,

(5) Blood does not show signs of ketosis,

(6) The blood–cholesterol and blood–triglyceride levels are normal,

(7) The amount of glycosylated haemoglobin is less than 8.5 per cent.

If the above-mentioned goals are not achieved with non-medicinal modes of treatment, the patient should, without delay, start medicines as per his doctor's advice.

Till the disease comes under total control and till the physical condition has stabilised, the patient has to visit his doctor frequently.

Once the correct amounts of diet, exercise and medicines have been arrived at, the patient should faithfully cling to the treatment programme. A person who has learned to administer an insulin injection himself and can analyse his own urine and blood need not usually visit his doctor before three-monthly intervals. Thus the expenditure for treatment is considerably reduced.

The diabetic should meticulously note down the results of his day to day urine and blood analysis in a diary or a calendar, a model of which has been presented on page 120.

Date	Concentration of Sugar in urine/blood					Treatment (time)	Symptoms of hypogly-cemia	Ohter Remarks (weight, B. P.,
	Early Morning	Before Lunch	After Lunch	Before Supper	After Supper	Oral drugs/Insulin	(time)	Exs., Calories, etc.)

Such a record gives a complete information about the degree of control of the disease and guides the doctor in deciding the future treatment-plan.

Education : Child or young diabetics find no difficulty at all in pursuing education. Their intelligence and memory are in no way inferior to those of other healthy students.

It is desirable that the class-teacher and a few close friends of the diabetic student know that he has the disease and also know about the symptoms of hypoglycemia.

Household chores : A diabetic women can easily do all the household work herself. She should refrain from visiting relatives too frequently, where she may have to give in to her host's insistence to eat or drink prohibited preparations.

If during an occasion, the diabetic women has to work more, the amount of medicine should be correspondingly decreased or the amount of food increased.

Job/Business : A diabetic can usually follow any kind of job or business to earn his living.

It would be desirable that a few of his colleagues know about his disease and the steps to be taken in an emergency.

Marriages, Parties, Restaurants, etc : A diabetic can take part in any function of his choice. Albeit, he should remain careful about his diet. It is natural that the host may, out of courtesy, insist on his having certain dishes or foods. But the diabetic should politely refuse, without making too much fuss. He should not hesitate to leave behind those sweet foods which have been forcibly placed in his plate.

Sport : Juvenile as well as adult diabetics can participate in sports, regularly or occasionally. However, care should be taken to prevent blood-sugar level from dropping too low. An untoward incident can be prevented by having immediately before the start of the sport, a snack which would provide easily and rapidly digestible carbohydrates.

Other illnesses : Like other people, diabetics, too, may suffer from other routine illnesses. Medicines taken for those illnesses may affect the blood-sugar level or may interfere with anti-diabetic drugs. For example, a drug called cortisone may elevate the blood-sugar level. If this drug is inevitable, the dosage of insulin must be proportionately increased for the time-being. Most tonics and cough syrups have considerable amounts of sugar and should be avoided by diabetics. In fact, a diabetic should take no medicine without his doctor's consent.

Driving a vehicle : Today, maintaining and driving a vehicle is a part of life. A diabetic should remain careful while driving.

It is desirable that patients whose blood-sugar level fluctuates wildly (unstable or brittle diabetes) refrain from driving. This would prevent an accident on the road.

A diabetic who has to drive for long periods of time, should have a suitable snack before commencing the drive. Besides, he should keep with him foods which would supply easily and rapidly digestible carbohydrates.

9 / Diabetes......Without Any Fear

Surgery : Many people harbour a false notion that diabetics cannot undergo a surgery without grave risks to their lives. In fact, any operation can be safely and successfully carried out if the diabetes is well controlled.

Sometimes, an acute complication of diabetes may necessitate an emergency surgery. A diabetic who has not taken due care to control his disease may find himself in a tight corner in such a situation. The surgeon has first to bring down the blood-sugar level before performing the surgery. This results in loss of valuable time. This is one more reason why diabetes should always be kept under strict control.

Pregnancy : At one time, diabetes was a grave risk factor for diabetic pregnant women. The incidence of abortion or death of either the child or the mother was very high. The discovery of insulin has considerably transformed the situation. Even then, it is not easy for a diabetic women to first conceive and then give birth to a healthy baby at the right time. Difficulties can however be kept to the minimum with an expert gynaecologist's care.

During pregnancy, the blood-sugar level of a diabetic woman fluctuates. In the first trimester of pregnancy, the requirement of insulin is low. During the second trimester of pregnancy, the blood-sugar level and consequently the requirement of insulin rises. If due care is not taken during this period, ketosis may ensue. In the last trimester of pregnancy, diabetes becomes very acute and management of the pregnant women poses great difficulties. Many a doctor opts for an early forced delivery, about two to three weeks before the right time.

During labour, a pregnant diabetic women has to strain a lot. Consequently her blood-sugar level plunges. Even after the delivery the blood-sugar level remains low for a few days, that is to say the disease seemingly disappears. This, however, proves to be a temporary relief and diabetes soon reappears.

The blood glucose level of certain women rises only during pregnancy. Such diabetes is termed 'diabetes of pregnancy'. Prior to conception and after the delivery, the blood-sugar values are normal. About 50 per cent of such women develop frank diabetes later in life. All women who present high blood-sugar levels during pregnancy or who give birth to large babies should take all possible steps to prevent frank diabetes in future.

In conclusion it can be said that a clear understanding of the disease and effective medicines available today enable the diabetic to lead an almost normal life. He can, under certain limits, play all sports, perform all activities and enjoy life. In many a country, there are special associations of diabetics, which arrange entertainment programmes and get-togethers for diabetics, hold sports competitions and keep the members appraised of new developments in the understanding and the treatment of the disease.

Great patriot Lokmanya Tilak and great saint Swami Vivekanand had diabetes. Talbert, the famous tennis player was a diabetic. Dr. Minot received the prestigious Nobel prize for medicine, in spite of suffering from diabetes. Prominent persons from all walks of life are living a joyous, active life in spite of diabetes.

Come, let us accept the challenge posed by diabetes. If we obtain a correct understanding of the disease, we need not fear it, nor need we allow it to interfere with our normal life.

Chapter in a nutshell :

1. Today, diabetics lead a long, happy and active life.
2. Diabetic children or youths find no difficulty in pursuing education. Their grasping power, memory and intelligence are in no way inferior to those of other students.

3. Diabetic women can perform all the household chores.
4. Diabetics can take up occupations of their choice to earn their living.
5. Diabetics can take part in almost all games and competitions.
6. Diabetics can, in fact, do everything that normal persons could do. They can enjoy all the pleasures in life.
7. The great philosopher Swami Vivekanand, the great patriot Lokmanya Tilak, nobel laureate Dr. Minot and tennis wizard Talbert were all diabetics. They beat all the odds to reach the top.

PART II : HIGH BLOOD PRESSURE

11. INTRODUCTION

One minute he was walking along, seemingly in the best of health. The very next moment, he was on the ground, clutching his chest and writhing with pain. They did get him to the hospital; but he died on the way. This young business-man, at the age of 43, was a victim, according to the death certificate, of myocardial infraction : heart attack. But this heart attack was just the end result or the terminal event of a process going on his body for many years, not the real cause.

* * *

Some one and a half months back he had a strange and frightful experience in his office. He was seated at his desk when the oppressive squeezing pressure beneath his chest bone came. He tried to stand up but his legs gave way. His secretary, who happened to walk in at that moment, realised the gravity of the situation and got him to a hospital. He was immediately admitted to the intensive cardiac care unit and was connected to a host of over-whelming instruments.

Some time later, his heart fibrillated, shivered and sud-denly stopped beating, rendering him unconscious. He was immediately attended to by alert doctors. Electrodes on his chest shocked the heart back to action.

When he regained consciousness, he was in the hospi-tal's coronary care unit, enmeshed in wires and tubes. For the next week, he was monitored and watched round the clock by specially trained personnel.

He recovered. After several weeks he was out of the hospital. His bill : more than 10,000 rupees. But he is one of the fortunate ones, to be back with his family again. Within a short period, he should be able to resume work.

The hospital case-records have noted down the diagnosis of his malady as 'a heart attack'.

But once again, the heart attack was not the prime cause but an end result of something else.

* * *

'I never fall ill , she used to say with pride. Until she sat down to dinner that night, she was hale and hearty. But suddenly, at the table, she became dizzy and confused. Dark clouds loomed large in front of her eyes. The spoon in her hand fell down upon the table. In a few moments, she was fine again, 'Mom was dozing' her children said jokingly. But she had not dozed. It was not a momentary sleep. Like thousands of other people, she had experienced a 'little stroke'. Over the next months, she suffered such other mild strokes, manifested by brief bouts of vertigo and numbness or moments of unconsciousness.

Then she woke up one morning, with one hand numb and awkward. Her tea cup slipped from her hands. Within the next thirty minutes, the right side of the body was paralysed—a big stroke! She had suffered from cerebral haemorrhage.

If she is lucky, she will survive it. If she is very lucky, she may regain a reasonable measure of her former ability to speak, move and live a normal life.

This bleeding into the brain was also an end result of a process going on in her body since years.

* * *

Disasters like heart attack, brain haemorrhage, kidney failure happen every moment, every day. And they strike suddenly. Before such an accident, the affected person had always considered himself to be a living example of health.

We blame the heart attack or the brain haemorrhage for the catastrophe. But the real culprit is another process, a silent disease or a fooler of a disease. This disease works insidiously inside the body, damaging most of the organs and the systems without producing a single symptom. The person, unaware of the process, considers himself at the peak of health. One gloomy day, the process suddenly and almost always unexpectedly surfaces and with a cruel blow, shatters the person's illusions about his good health.

This process is **high blood pressure, a hard but quietly hard pounding of blood.** Medically it is termed as hypertension. Hypertension should not be confused with mental tension or nervousness.

As per the extensive surveys carried out in a number of countries, almost 25 per cent of the population is trapped in the clutches of high blood pressure; and the incidence is rapidly rising.

History has noted that renowned physician Dr. William Harvey, internationally acclaimed scientists Edward Jenner, Richard Bright and Louis Pasteur, great leaders Woodrow Wilson, Franklin Roosevelt and Joseph Stalin and many other public figures had to leave this world due to high blood pressure. Our beloved leader Jawaharlal Nehru and towering scientist Dr. Vikram Sarabhai, too, were victims of high blood pressure.

However, it should not be inferred that high blood pressure affects only the public figures. In fact, it makes no distinction between a king and a pauper, a public figure and a layman, a male and a female, the young and the aged. It strikes persons from all walks of life.

It is precisely for this reason that a clear understanding of the disease should be obtained. Only then can it be prevented or successfully controlled.

Fortunately, the present treatment for high blood pressure is quite effective and enables the victim to lead a long and happy life.

Chapter in a nutshell :

1. High blood pressure is a silent disease. It remains in the body without producing symptoms for years.

2. Many a time, it is detected only after one of its complications (e.g., a heart attack or an attack of paralysis) strikes.

3. This disease makes no distinction between the rich and the poor, the old and the young or a man and a woman.

---

12. WHAT DOES 'BLOOD PRESSURE' MEAN ?

'Blood pressure' is a mysterious word for lay people. However, it is not really so.

Blood pressure is merely the pressure that the blood exerts on the blood vessels, while circulating.

Blood pressure is essential for –

(1) the return of the blood to the heart, after making its way through more than 60,000 miles long blood vessels of our body, (2) the exchange of nutrients and waste products between the various cells of the body and the blood capillaries, (3) the filtering (and therefore purification) of blood in the kidneys and the lungs.

Stephen Hales, an English clergyman was the first person to try to measure the blood pressure. He used to securely tie a horse upside down and insert a long glass tube into its chief artery, the aorta. He observed that because of the pressure, the blood rose inside the tube, to a height of almost nine feet. That was in the fourth decade of the eighteenth century, 1733 A.D. to be precise.

Almost a hundred years later, in 1828 A.D., a French medical student Jean Leonard Poiseuille thought of connecting a mercury-filled U-tube to the aorta. Since mercury is 13.6 times heavier than blood or water, the column in the tube was raised to a much smaller height and indoor measurement of blood pressure became feasible. Even then, the method was obviously unsuitable to measure human blood pressure because an artery of a living person cannot be punctured. However, it should be noted that Poiseuille's idea of using mercury while measuring blood pressure is taken advantage of, even today. Almost all accurate instruments for measuring blood pressure incorporate mercury. Since Poiseuille's time, millimeters of mercury, or mm Hg, have been the standard units of blood pressure measurement.

It was to be almost 70 years before an Italian physician Scipion Rivorokki invented a measuring instrument which had an arm-cuff. This solved the problem of artery-puncture. Rivorokki argued, and rightly so, that the pressure of the arm-cuff that stops the flow of blood into the forearm, should be equivalent to the blood-pressure. The arm-cuff was connected to two things : to an air-pump and to a mercury-filled tube. Rivorokki first snugly tied the cuff around a person's arm. He then placed his fingers on the wrist of the person, where he could feel the pulsations (of the blood) in the 'radial' artery. Finally, with the air-pump he used to build up pressure inside the arm-cuff. He would consider that pressure (as observed in the mercury-filled tube) as the blood-pressure which made the pulsations in the radial artery to stop. Rivorokki did not realise that this was only the pressure of the blood while the heart was contracting.

Finally in 1905 A.D., a Russian physician Nicolai Korotcoff, using the stethoscope (the instrument which decorates the doctros' ears or necks), measured both the pressures i.e., when the heart was fully contracted and when the heart was fully relaxed.

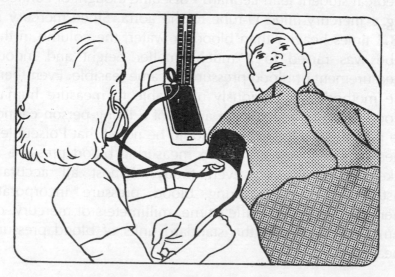

Fig. 12.1 : The sphygmomanometer

When the rythmically beating heart contracts, it forcefully drives the blood into the arteries. The pressure at such a time is high and is termed 'systolic blood pressure'. When the heart relaxes, the pressure is comparatively low and is termed 'diastolic blood pressure'. The instrument used to measure blood pressure is called a 'sphygmomanometer'.

A systolic blood pressure of 120 mm Hg and a diastolic blood pressure of 80 mm Hg are considered normal. These pressures are denoted as 120/80.

Blood pressure does not remain the same throughout the day; it undergoes slight variations (termed diurnal variations). The pressure is least during the early hours of the day, when a person is deep asleep. At around 9.00–9.30 a.m., the pressure is usually the maximum. Besides, the blood pressure is temporarily raised (many a time markedly so) by physical labour, mental strain, acute pain or fear.

It is essential that before measuring the blood pressure, the person should be made to rest for a while.

How is the blood pressure maintained?

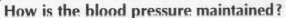

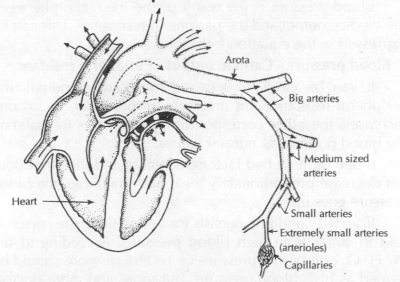

Arota

Big arteries

Medium sized arteries

Heart

Small arteries

Extremely small arteries (arterioles)

Capillaries

Fig. 12.2 : The heart and the arteries

Heart is a wonderful natural pump, made up of special muscles. It incessantly and rythmically beats, thereby maintaining the blood-circulation. Usually, it beats 72 times a minute. This number is termed, the 'heart rate'. At every contraction, the heart pumps about 70 ml (half a cup) of blood into the arteries. This quantity is termed, the **'stroke volume'.** Thus it pumps about 5 litres of blood every minute. This quantity is termed, the **'cardiac output'.** This can be expressed in the equation form thus :

Cardiac output = Stroke volume × Heart rate

The main artery, the aorta, arising from the heart divides into branches. These branches, in turn, give rise to smaller and smaller arteries. Such branching finally gives rise to extremely small arteries called 'arterioles'. The walls of the arterioles possess muscle fibres. The arterioles can, therefore, contract or expand as per the bodily needs. Usually the arterioles possess a tone i.e., they remain in a partially contracted state, thus slowing down the flow of blood. Such resistance to the flow of blood by the arterioles is called **'peripheral resistance'.**

Blood pressure is the result of the interaction between the cardiac output and the peripheral resistance. This can be expressed in the equation form thus :

Blood pressure = Cardiac output × Peripheral resistance

It can be easily understood that cardiac output and peripheral resistance are inversely proportional, i.e., if one increases, the other correspondingly decreases to maintain the blood pressure at normal values.

If one of these two factors increases and the other does not decrease proportionately (or if both increase), the blood pressure goes up.

If such a condition persists for a long time, the person is said to suffer from high blood pressure. According to the W. H. O. criterion, a pressure of 160/95 or more should be termed as high blood pressure. But more and more doctors now consider 140/90 also as high blood pressure. In fact, lower the pressure, the better for a person. The words of Dr. William Kannel, director of the world-renowned

'Framingham Heart Study' are suggestive. He says, "An ideal blood pressure would be the lowest pressure you could achieve without going into a shock. People with low blood pressure may sometimes complain that they feel tired all the time, but they live for 120 years".

High blood pressure is of two types :

(1) Essential (simple) and (2) Secondary.

Secondary high blood pressure is caused by some other disease or disorder in the body.

More than 90 per cent of patients suffer from 'essential' hypertension. How essential hypertension develops, i.e., what changes or mechanisms in the body are responsible for elevation of the pressure, is not clearly understood. On the basis of research and experiments, scientists point towards certain mechanisms. However, these are very complicated and need not be dwelled on in detail.

Chapter in a nutshell :

1. Blood pressure is simply the pressure which the circulating blood exerts on the wall of the blood vessels.

2. The pressure on the wall of the blood vessels increases when the heart contracts; it decreases when the heart expands. The two pressures are termed normal if they are 120 and 80, respectively. This normal blood pressure is denoted as 120/80.

3. The blood pressure is measured with an instrument called sphygmomanometer.

4. The blood pressure depends upon two inversely proportional factors, i.e., the cardiac output and the arteriolar resistance. If one of these two factors increases and the other does not decrease proportionately, the blood pressure rises.

5. There are two varieties of high blood pressure : simple (essential) and secondary. Almost 90 per cent of patients suffer from the simple variety of this disorder.

---

13. THE AETIOLOGY OF HIGH BLOOD PRESSURE

It has been mentioned earlier that high blood pressure results from an imbalance between the cardiac output and the peripheral resistance.

The following factors may, independently or in conjunction, lead to such an imbalance.

(1) Heredity : Most experts believe that heredity does play a role in causing high blood pressure. That the incidence of this disease is double than normal in kins of persons with high blood pressure, is suggestive.

Fig. 13.1

A few researchers believe that it is not the heredity but environmental factors which cause high blood pressure. Children imitate the dietary habits and life style or their elders. Consequently they, too, suffer from disorders which their parents are afflicted with.

In what way and to what extent do hereditory factors act is still not clear. As for diabetes, it can be said for high blood pressure too that 'In the development of high blood pressure, heredity loads the cannon and environmental factors pull the trigger.' In short, if exciting environmental forces are not at play, heredity can have little influence.

(2) **Mental tension and approach** : All researchers accept the role of mental tension and negative thinking in the development of high blood pressure.

In an experiment, too many mice were forced into a single cage. This overcrowding led to mental tension in mice which in turn led to high blood pressure. If such a situation was allowed to stay for some time, the high blood pressure became established, i.e., the pressure did not drop even ater the mice were removed from the cage.

Mental tension leads to excessive secretion of catecholamines (adrenaline and nor-adrenaline) inside the body. These secretions undesirably stimulate the catecholaminergic nerve endings in the brain-stem to cause an elevation of the blood pressure.

The incidence of high blood pressure in too ambitious, too much self-controlled or emotion-throttling (who consciously refrain from expressing their feelings) and workoholic persons, has been found to be much higher.

Deep studies and widespread surveys have shown that persons with a particular type of personality or behaviour-pattern suffer from high blood pressure more often. Scientists have named such behaviour : 'type A behaviour'. Type A behaviour has clear cut characteristics. A person with type A behaviour —

(1) talks aggressively and hurriedly; he unnecessarily stresses or accentuates certain words while speaking and hurries the ends of the sentences,

(2) always moves, walks and eats rapidly,

(3) becomes impatient if events taking place in front of his eyes are slow; he strives to rapidly complete the sentences of others, thinking they speak too slowly or not to the point,

(4) gets irritated and enraged if the vehicle in front is moving slowly,

(5) gets impatient or irritated if he has to stand in a queue,

(6) gets irritated if a work is being done slowly, which he thinks he could have done faster,

(7) tries to accomplish more than one work at one time; he reads the newspaper while having his lunch or eats his morning breakfast while shaving,

(8) prefers to go through the summary of a book instead of reading it fully,

(9) always dwells in his own thoughts; while with others, he tries to bring the theme of the conversation to those subjects which especially interest and intrigue him and if unable to accomplish this maneouver, pretends to listen but remains preoccupied with his own thoughts.

(10) feels vaguely guilty if he has nothing to do even for a while; he just cannot enjoy a weekend or a vacation,

(11) attempts to schedule more and more in less and less time, leaving little room for unseen contingencies; in short, he sufferes from a chronic sense of time-urgency,

(12) feels challenged or jealous when in company of another 'type A' person,

(13) unconsciously clinches his fists or jaws and grinds his teeth, while occupied in some work,

(14) thinks that his success depends solely upon the pace of his work,

(15) tries to accomplish most tasks in the same vein, hesitates to employ a new idea or a new system and lacks imagination and creativity,

(16) cannot remember the colour or furniture of even a most recently visited place; knows little about his neighbours, nearby shops or other places,

(17) considers it to be a waste of time if he has to play with his children on returning home from work,

(18) remains so engrossed in his activity that is unaware of things occurring around him,

(19) has an extreme fascination for numbers; if a businessman, he is more interested in the figure of his income than in how he will use that money.

Even with a fleeting glance at the above list, it is clear that a 'type A' person considers life a battle, races against the clock and invites mental tension.

In an experiment, psychologists analysed the minds of thousands of college students to classify them into 'type A' and 'non type A' personalities. Thereafter, the psychologists predicted that most of the 'type A' students will develop high blood pressure over the years. This prediction turned out to be absolutely true. That 'non type A' students did not develop high blood pressure is suggestive.

The reader is strongly recommended to analyse his mind on the basis of above characteristics of 'type A' behaviour.

Mental tension or 'type A' personality stimulates the secretion of certain undesirable juices inside the body, which increase the arteriolar resistance and cause high blood pressure.

It would not be an exaggeration to say that a 'type A' person literally rushes towards high blood pressure and coronary heart disease.

(3) **Excessive intake of salt :** That an excessive intake of common salt (sodium chloride) elevates the blood pressure is an indisputable fact.

Extensive studies have shown that in all those countries where the average salt-intake is high, the incidence of high blood pressure, too, is high. Even in a single country, the incidence of high blood pressure is higher in coastal places than in the interiors.

Several thousand Americans were studied, between 1950 and 1952 A.D., to determine the relationship between the salt-intake and high blood pressure. People were divided into three groups : (1) those consuming 2 – 3 grams of salt a day, (2) those consuming 4 to 10 grams of salt a day and (3) those consuming 12 to 18 grams of salt a day. This study showed that the blood pressure of low salt eaters remained almost normal even in old age; people whose salt- consumption was more that 5 grams a day had a high incidence of high blood pressure.

In fact, salt is just an old habit of human beings. The salt contents of natural foods is remarkably low. It is the man who adds salt to food at every step. We ourselves make our children addicts of common salt. We may prefer to remain hungry to taking saltless diet. But we should note that those who have never tasted salt, find its taste extremely disagreeable.

(4) **Obesity (excessive weight) :** The relationship between obesity and high blood pressure is well known.

High blood pressure is extremely common in fat persons. On the basis of a study of 567 obese and 1225 normal persons, Dr. Pincherle and Dr. Wright have shown that the incidence of high blood pressure is $2\frac{1}{2}$ times more in obese than in normal persons.

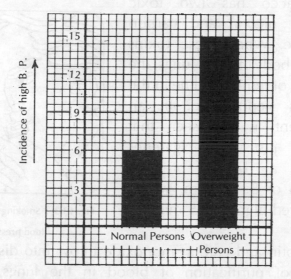

Fig. 13.2 : Obesity and high blood pressure

After examining 74000 industrial workers, Drs. Master, Dublin and Marks found that the blood pressure is proportional to body-weight. The greater the obesity, the higher is the blood pressure. Another alarming fact is that in the obese, high pressure develops much earlier in life, sometimes even in the second decade.

(5) **Sedentary life :** The incidence of high blood pressure is much higher in sedentary persons than in physical labourers.

In a study covering 1000 athletes, it was found that they had a systolic blood pressure of only 99 mm Hg on an average.

(6) **Smoking :** The incidence of high blood pressure has been found to be higher in smokers. Smokers more often fall victims to atherosclerosis, heart attack and cerebral haemorrhage.

Tobacco has two toxic elements : nicotin and carbon monoxide. When these toxins enter the body through lungs, the secretion of noradrenaline in the blood is stepped up. In an experiment, it was seen that smoking just two cigarettes causing a blood pressure elevation of 8–10 mm, which then stayed high for 15 minutes or more.

Fig. 13.3 : Smoking and high blood pressure

Nicotin and carbon monoxide throw into disarray the process of purification of blood in the lungs, thereby burdening the heart.

(7) **Alcohol consumption :** Studies conducted in America, Britain, Sweden, Australia and a number of other countries have proved that the incidence of high blood pressure in drinkers is $2\frac{1}{2}$ times higher than that in non-drinkers.

Chapter in a nutshell :

1. Scientists have pointed towards the possible causes of high blood pressure.
2. The role of heredity as a causative factor has been universally acknowledged.
3. If exciting environmental factors like faulty mental attitude (type A behaviour), excessive salt-intake, obesity, sedentary life, smoking and alcohol consumption are not present, heredity cannot have its influence.

References :

1. Pincherle, G., Wright, H. – Screening in the early diagnosis and prevention of cardiovascular disease, J. Coll. Gen. Practit., 13 : 280, 1967.

2. Master, A. M., Dublin, L. I., Marks, H. H. – The normal blood pressure range and its clinical implementations, J. A. M. A., 143 : 1464, 1950.

3. Christakis, G. et al – A nutritional epidemiologic investigation of 642 New York City Children, Am. J. Clin. Nutr., 21 : 107, 1968.

14. HAZARDS OF HIGH BLOOD PRESSURE

Uptil the beginning of this century, physicians considered high blood pressure a good development. They knew that with ageing, the blood vessels become narrow and hard. A high pressure, according to them, was necessary to force the blood through the narrowed vessels. They believed that if blood pressure was brought down, important organs would receive less blood, with grave consequences.

Between 1903 and 1912 A.D., Dr. Janeway studied 8000 patients to show that high blood pressure reduces the life span. In 1934 A.D., Dr. Page proved that nutrition to different organs is not cut down by lowering the elevated blood pressure.

Today, high blood pressure has been nicknamed 'a silent killer' and rightly so. It lies in the body without giving rise to any symptom for years and damages the various organs.

The risks of high blood pressure are as follows :

(1) Atherosclerosis (hardening of the blood vessels) : The blood vessels of a healthy person are highly elastic. This property of elasticity is extremely essential because organs require less or more blood as per the need of the situation. For example, heart requires more blood when a person is doing a strenuous activity. At such a time, the coronary arteries expand so as to carry more blood to the heart.

High blood pressure renders the blood vessel narrow and hard. The proof to this claim is the fact that pulmonary arteries, where the blood pressure is as low as 35/15, never develop atherosclerosis.

Narrow and hardened arteries cannot expand to carry more blood even when necessary. Chest pain (angina pectoris) arises when coronary arteries supplying nutrition to the heart do not expand during physical activity.

If the process of atherosclerosis progresses unabated, a coronary artery may become too narrow and may get totally obstructed. This results into the death of a part the heart muscle. This is nothing but a heart attack. Of all the victims of a heart attack, almost 75 per cent confess of having suffered from high blood pressure for some time.

Mortality rate following a heart attack is four times higher in persons with high blood pressure than in others.

Atherosclerosis also renders the blood vessels brittle. If a brittle brain-artery ruptures, brain haemorrhage follows. This is termed a 'stroke'. Stroke may lead to paralysis or even instant death.

(2) **Heart failure** : When blood pressure is high, the heart has to overwork.

To perform the increased work, the heart muscle thickens and increases in size. This enlargement of heart is visible on X-ray pictures. The phenomenon is much like what happens to a muscle which is exercised strenuously and constantly, for example, the bicep muscle on the front side of the arm; its girth increases.

For a period of time, despite the increased workload, the heart does well. It accommodates and handles the burden. But there comes a time when it tires and is unable to fully meet the strain. The result is congestive heart failure.

In heart failure, the heart does not stop beating. It continues to beat but its contractions are no longer as complete and effective. With each contraction, less volume of blood is pumped.

There are many effects of loss of pumping efficiency or heart failure. Since less blood reaches the tissues of the body, muscles suffer from lack of adequate nourishment and there is muscle fatigue. Less blood may reach the brain and the patient may not be able to think as effectively as he previously could.

There is a build-up of pressure within the heart itself. Unable to pump out blood completely, the heart experiences increased internal pressure as its chambers dilate and become reservoirs for abnormal amounts of blood. The pressure extends backwards to the lungs, which may then retain fluids, sometimes as much as several litres. From the lungs the pressure is transmitted still further back to the veins of the body, the liver and the legs. The liver becomes congested and enlarged; the legs swell with fluids; the neck veins become distended.

In spite of vigorous treatment, 50 per cent of persons suffering from heart failure do not survive for more than five years; and 20 per cent of them leave for the heavenly abode within a year.

(3) **Detrimental effects on kidneys :** If the blood pressure is elevated, the kidneys cannot perform their work of blood-filtration effectively. Consequently salt and toxins accumulate in the body. Each gram of salt accumulated in the body has a capacity to hold back 70 grams of water from being excreted. Such water retention aggrevates heart failure.

High blood pressure also gradually destroys the cells of the kidneys. Kidney damage is manifested by loss of useful nutrients through the urine. A study conducted by Dr. Perera showed that 42 per cent of people who did nothing to control their blood pressure, lost albumin in their urine. Statistics show that unless vigorously and incessantly treated, persons losing albumin in their urine do not survive for more than five years.

(4) **Arteriolar inflammation :** Some patients of high blood pressure suffer from inflammation of the arterioles. The cells of the walls of the arterioles undergo necrosis and destruction. The symptoms of this disorder include rapidly increasing high blood pressure (accelerated hypertension), retinal haemorrhages and progressive kidney failure. There was a time when arteriolar inflammation led to an almost certain death within an year. Today, however, a patient's life can be prolonged with effective drugs.

(5) **Dissecting aneurysm of the aorta :** A part of the main artery (aorta) becomes thin in some patients of high blood pressure. The cells of the thinned part undergo rotting and destruction. The thinned part may then balloon out either outwards or inwards (into the lumen of the aorta). If it balloons inwards, it obstructs the flow of blood. If it balloons outwards it may rupture, causing massive haemorrhage. If the condition is immediately diagnosed, the patient's life may be saved by drugs and an operation; if not, death soon ensues.

(6) **Reduced life-expectancy :** The most serious hazard of high blood pressure is that it shortens life.

For example, for a man of 35, if the blood pressure is 142/85, the mortality rate is 150 per cent above average; if the blood pressure is 152/85, the mortality rate increases to 225 per cent; if the blood pressure is 145/95, the mortality rate is again 225 per cent above average; if the blood pressure is 152/95, the mortality rate increases to 300 per cent above average.

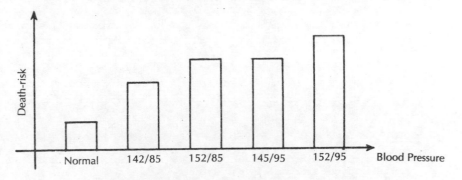

Fig. 14.1 : High blood pressure and life-expectancy

This sixth risk factor indicates that however mild the elevation of blood pressure, zealous efforts should be made to bring it down, without delay.

Chapter in a nutshell :

1. High blood pressure has been nicknamed 'a silent killer' and rightly so. It produces no symptoms but quietly and insidiously harms the organs and the systems of the body.

2. High blood pressure renders the blood vessels narrow, hard and brittle. This disorder is termed atherosclerosis.

3. Heart attack, heart failure, kidney failure and cerebral haemorrhage are the natural consequences of high blood pressure.

4. High blood pressure actually shortens life and drags its victim to a premature death.

References :

1. Janeway, T. C.—A clinical study of hypertensive cardiovascular disease, Arch. Intern. Med., 12 : 755–798, 1913.

2. Page, I. H.—The effects on renal efficiency of lowering arterial blood pressure in cases of essential hypertension and nephritis, J. Clin. Invest., 13 : 909–915, 1934.

3. Perera, G. A. —Hypertensive vascular disease; description and natural history, J. Chronic Disease, 1 : 33–42, 1955.

15. HIGH BLOOD PRESSURE : SYMPTOMS AND DIAGNOSIS

It is commonly believed that high blood pressure is a malady of old age and mainly afflicts males. This belief is, however, not totally correct.

The incidence of high blood pressure (140/90 or more) has been found to be as high as 10 to 11 per cent in children and youths. It rises to 20–25 per cent in the middle aged. The possibility of a person above 50, developing high blood pressure afresh, is very slight indeed.

That women suffer from high blood pressure less commonly is a partially true belief. Though it is true that the incidence of high blood pressure in menstruating women is lower than that in men, after menopause it increases to equal that in men, In fact, a survey indicates that the incidence of high blood pressure in women older than 65 years, is actually higher than that in men.

The belief that high blood pressure afflicts only the affluent class is also not wholly true. This disease does not differenciate between the rich and the poor, high society and low society. However, in America, more blacks have high blood pressure than the whites.

People believe that a person with high blood pressure commonly suffers from headache, burning of eyes, giddiness, palpitations, nose-bleedings, distended veins and that he can immediately be recognised from his flushed face. But this belief has not even a grain of truth in it.

In fact, high blood pressure produces no symptoms at all; at least not in the early stages. That is the reason why it is termed a hidden disease or a silent killer.

In most patients, high blood pressure is diagnosed accidentally, usually during a physical examination undertaken for some other disease or for an insurance policy. In quite a few patients, it is diagnosed only after one of its complication (e.g., chest pain, a heart attack, a stroke or kidney failure) presents itself.

Most patients start getting headaches only after they are told that they have high blood pressure!

It should be noted that no doctor can or should proclaim the verdict of high blood pressure to a person after only a single measurement of blood pressure. The diagnosis of high blood pressure can only be made if the blood pressure is found elevated on two or more separate occasions.

Before diagnosing the high blood pressure as of the essential (simple) variety, all the causes of secondary high blood pressure should be excluded. The more common causes, symptoms and treatment of secondary high blood pressure have been tabulated on page 149.

	Cause/Type	Symptoms	Investigations	Treatment
1	Co-arctation (kinking) of the aorta	Headache, weakness of leg muscles, varicose veins on the back and waist, etc. The blood pressure in arm-arteries is high but that in leg-arteries is normal or low.	X ray, E C G	Surgery
2	A disorder of kidney/s (e.g., glomerulonephritis, pyelonephritis, systemic lupus arythymatosus, poly-arteritis nodosa, polycystic kidney, renal artery stenosis, etc.)	Onset in very young or very old age; pain in the abdomen and the back ; peculiar sounds (bruits) in the abdomen on ascultation; an absence of family history.	Urine, I. V. P., etc.	In some disorders surgery may help
3	Hormonal imbalance or long term use of hormone drugs (disorders include pheochromocytoma, Cushing's syndrome, aldosteronism and use of contraceptive pills)	History of consumption of contraceptive pills; excessive muscle- weakness; hair on the face in women; moon-like face, etc. Patients with pheochromocytoma get attacks of sweating and headache	X Ray photographs of bones; chemical tests to determine the concentrations of hormones in the blood; urine analysis to determine concentrations of V. M. A.; X-Ray abdomen	Stop using contraceptive pills or hormone drugs; In some disorders; surgery or medicines may help
4	Pregnancy (pressure becomes high in only some pregnant women, not all)	None except elevation of pressure	None	Medicines
5	Long term use of drugs called mono-amino oxidase inhibitors.	None except elevation of pressure	None	Stop using the culprit drugs.

Chapter in a nutshell :

1. Men as well as women, old as well as young and rich as well as poor are afflicted by high blood pressure.

2. There are no symptoms of high blood pressure! In most patients, it is diagnosed accidentally or only after one of its complication (e.g., a heart attack or an attack of paralysis) presents itself.

3. A person should be termed a patient of high blood pressure only if his blood pressure is found to be elevated on two or three separate occasions.

16. TREATMENT OF HIGH BLOOD PRESSURE

If the blood pressure is not very high, it can usually be controlled by non-medical treatment.

Even those patients for whom medicines are necessary, cannot do away with other non-medical measures. Such non-medical measures work to keep the dosage of medicines to the minimum. This obviously minimises the risk of side-effects. This fact is especially important for persons with high blood pressure because treatment for this disorder is to be continued throughout the life.

Non-medical modes of treatment

(1) **Change your outlook and the life-style :** High blood pressure is a result of modern, fast and competitive life. Persons with type A behaviour invariably attract this disease.

If you possess a type A personality, straightaway implement efforts to change your mental attitude. This may be difficult; but it is not impossible. Understand and accept the 'Theory of Karma'. Work hard, but do not long for returns. Do not compete with the clock. Make no resolutions like 'I should complete all these works by today', or 'I should finish this work within this much time'. Do not take office-work to your home. Give some time of the day to your parents, your wife and your children. Let Sunday remain a resting day. Enjoy a 2 – 3 weeks vacation every year.

To decrease mental tension and regain inner peace, resort to Pranayama, Vipashyna, Transcendental Meditation or Biofeedback.

(2) **Restrict salt-intake :** The connection between high blood pressure and high salt-intake is well known. Therefore, in this disorder, drastically cutting down the salt-intake is indispensable. We usually consume 10-15 grams of salt everyday. This quantity should be cut down to a mere 2 – 3 grams.

(A) Use a minimum amount of salt while cooking.

(B) Never use salt at the table.

(C) Never consume processed or canned foods because they abound in salt.

(D) Refrain from eating pickles, chutneys and papads.

(E) Drastically cut down the consumption of salted peanuts, wafers, potato-chips, etc.

(F) Eat only salt-free biscuits.

(G) Do not buy butter or cheese from the market; they contain a lot of salt.

Understand clearly that other modes of treatment, including drugs, will be rendered ineffective if you continue to consume salt recklessly.

Common salt can be substituted by potassium salt (K – salt). In fact, things like mustard seeds, pepper and lemon juice can lend great taste to the food and make us unaware of the absence of salt.

(3) **Reduce your weight if you are obese** : High blood pressure and obesity are intimately related. Many a time, the blood pressure drops merely by reducing weight.

Determine the ideal body-weight for your height and body-frame from the tables given at the end of this book. If your weight is more than ideal, immediately make efforts to reduce it.

(4) **Do exercises and yogasanas regularly** : That light exercises and yogasanas reduce blood pressure is a proven fact.

It should be noted that only isotonic exercises (those which are repetitive and which are done at a constant pace) are beneficial. Such exercises include walking, jogging, swimming, cycling, etc. Isometric exercises, which require a person to use a lot of force in spurts (e.g., weight-lifting) do more harm than good.

Exercises should not be overdone.. A person should choose exercises according to his age and his stamina.

Yogasanas are extremely beneficial to patients of high blood pressure. Dr. Udupa of Banaras Hindu University's Institute of Medical Sciences tried selected yogasanas (especially Shavasana) on 25 patients, whose high blood pressure could not be brought down by other means. These patients were continuously monitored and their blood and urine samples periodically examined. Laboratory investigations resorted to, included plasma catecholamine level, plasma cortisol level and urinary V. M. A. level. At the end of three months, there`was a notable reduction in all these three factors, besides the blood pressure. The results have been tabulated below[1] :

No.	Investigation	Before treatment	After treatment (yogasanas)
1	Blood pressure	152/102	139/90
2	Plasma catecholamine	289.82	234.91
3	Plasma cortisol	27.49	25.02
4	Urinary VMA	2.48	2.05

Dr. Udupa considers Shavasana to be extremely beneficial in high blood pressure. Besides, other asanas like Padmasana, Vajrasana, Yogamudra, Dhanurasana, Paschimottanasana, Konasana, Matsyasana and Matsyendrasana should be learnt from a good teacher or a good book and practised regularly.

All such asanas in which the body is held upside down (e.g., Sarvangasana, Shirshasana) are prohibited in high blood pressure.

(5) **Cultivate correct dietary habits :** All the suggestions for diabetics regarding the type and the amount of diet are applicable to persons with high blood pressure too.

A person with high blood pressure should consume a low-sugar, low-saturated fat, low-salt and low-calorie diet.

Calcium and potassium have also been found to be useful to bring down blood pressure. Drs. MacGregor, Parfrey, McCarron and Belizan have performed innumerable experiments to prove this fact. [2, 3, 4, 5] The natural sources of these two minerals have been listed at the end of this book.

Besides, a vitamin-like substance choline also reduces blood pressure. Dr. Hartroff, Dr. Nishizawa and nobel laureate Dr. Best have obtained good results with choline in the treatment of high blood pressure [6, 7, 8]

The yellow of the egg, meat, yeast, soyabeans, germinated wheat, peas, beans, groundnuts, cabbage, spinach and mustard are good sources of choline. Of these, vegetable sources are preferable since meat and eggs are rich in saturated fats.

(6) **Abandon alcohol :** The relationship between high blood pressure and alcohol consumption has been proved by many workers.

It is a proven fact that blood pressure comes down in a few days after a person gives up drinking. If a person continues to drink, other measures to reduce blood pressure usually fail. [9]

(7) **Stop smoking :** That tobacco speeds up atherosclerosis is an undeniable fact. How high blood pressure and atherosclerosis ruin the heart and the kidneys, has been discussed previously.

It is not only desirable but very essential that a person wanting to bring down his blood pressure, should stop smoking completely.

(8) **Give Magnet Therapy a chance :** It has been seen that many a person with high blood pressure are benefitted by Magnet Therapy.

The blood pressure gradually comes down if the right wrist is treated with the north pole (or both the poles) of magnets. Belts, which can be worn on the wrist are also available. They are more convenient.

Besides, a north pole may be applied below the right ear, over the carotid artery, for 15 – 15 minutes twice a day.

Drinking water influenced by strong magnets also helps.

(9) **Give Acupressure a chance :** Good results have been obtained by Acupressure treatment, in mild or moderate high blood pressure. The systolic blood pressure comes down rapidly after initiating Acupressure treatment. But the diastolic blood pressure comes down gradually. Besides, it may not come down to the desired level. However, Acupressure has enabled quite a few patients to cut down the dosage of antihypertensive drugs by 33 to 50 per cent[10]. This is also a big gain.

The following Acupressure points should be used :

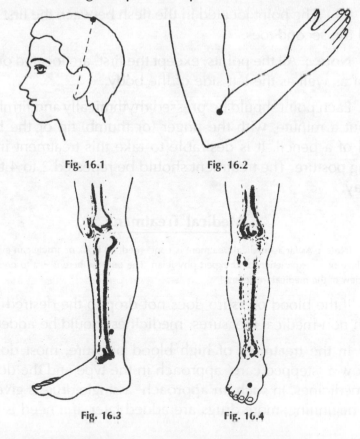

Fig. 16.1   Fig. 16.2

Fig. 16.3   Fig. 16.4

Description of these points :

(1) The point located on the middle of an imaginary vertical line joining the two ears after they have been folded forward.

(2) The point located on the outer end of the elbow crease formed due to bending of the elbow.

(3) The point located four fingerbreadths above the inner prominence of the ankle bone and slightly to the backside.

(4) The point located four fingerbreadths below the lower margin of the round knee-bone and slightly to the outer side, after the knee has been bent at a right angle.

(5) The point located in the flesh between the first (big) and the second toes.

Note : All the points, except the first, are located on the right as well as the left side of the body.

Each point should be pressed rhythmically and firmly for about a minute, with the finger (or thumb) tip or the blunt end of a pencil. It is desirable to take this treatment in the lying posture. The treatment should be repeated 2 to 4 times a day.

Medical Treatment

(**Note :** As far as medical treatment is concerned, no book or article can ever take the place of an experienced and expert physician. The purpose here is just to present an overview of the medical treatment.)

If the blood pressure does not drop to the desired level with non-medical measures, medicines should be added.

In the treatment of high blood pressure, most doctors follow a 'stepped care' approach in the type and the dosage of medicines. In such an approach, a single drug is given in the beginning; more drugs are added later, if a need is felt.

The following drugs are commonly used to treat high blood pressure :

(1) Diuretics

(2) Sympathetic inhibitors

(A) Beta blockers (e.g., Propanolol, Nadolol, Metoprolol, Atinolol, Timolol, Pindolol, Acebutolol)

(B) Central alpha – adrenergic agonists (e.g., Methyl dopa, Clonidine, Guanabenz)

(C) Catecholamine depleting agents (e.g., Reserpine)

(D) Post-synaptic alpha-adrenergic blockers (e.g., prazosin)

(E) Post-ganglionic sympathetic inhibitors (e.g., Guanithidine, Guanadrel)

(F) Vasodilators (e.g., Hydralazine, Minoxidil).

Whether the treatment should be begun with a diuretic drug or a Beta blocker drug is a matter of personal choice. Opinions differ. Mostly a diuretic is given in the beginning. After commencing with this medical treatment, the patient's blood pressure is monitored for 4 to 6 weeks. The blood pressure of most patients gets controlled by this drug. A betablocker drug is tried on the rest. It has, however, been seen that a combination of a diuretic and a betablocker drug is more effective than any of these drugs used singly. Besides, when used in conjunction, the total dosage of these drugs is much lesser than that of a single drug. This is an advantage since chances of side-effects are minimised.

If the blood pressure does not come down satisfactorily with the above two drugs, most doctors add either methyldopa or clonidine as the third drug.

If the blood pressure is very high (or when a critical condition ensues), medicines like Prazosin, Hydralazine or Minoxidil may have to be added.

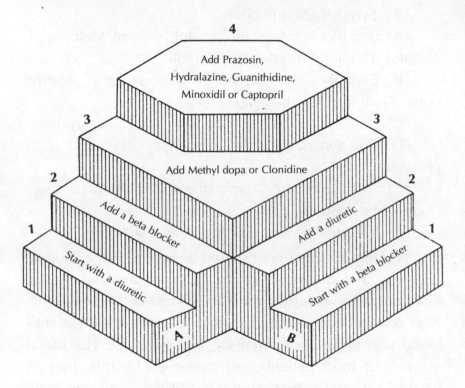

Fig. 16.5 : The 'stepped care' approach in the medical treatment of high blood pressure

No person with high blood pressure should ever think that medicines allow him to take liberties with diet and exercise. Even after starting medicines, non-medicinal modes of treatment are inevitable and should be persisted with.

Chapter in a nutshell :

1. The treatment of high blood pressure should be continued throughout the life, with great zeal and perseverence.

2. After the diagnosis of high blood pressure, initially non-medical modes of treatment should be given a try. By bringing about changes in the mental attitude and the life style, by restricting the intake of salt, by cultivating correct dietary habits, by giving up smoking and alcohol and by employing Magnet therapy and Acupressure, the blood pressure of many a patient can be adequately controlled.

3. If non-medical measures do not yield satisfactory results, medicines should be added to the treatment.

References :

1. K. N. Udupa, M. S., F. R. C.S., F. A. C. S., F. A. M. S. – Stress and its Management by Yoga, Motilal Banarsidass, Delhi, 1985.

2. MacGregor, D.A., Smith, S. J. et al – Moderate potassium supplementation in essential hypertension, Lancet, 1982; 2 : 567–570.

3. Parfrey, P. S., Wright, P. et al – Blood pressure and hormonal changes following alteration in dietary sodium and potassium in mild essential hypertension, Lancet, 1981; 1 : 59–63.

4. McCarron, D. A., Morris, C. D., Cole, C. – Dietary calcium in human hypertension, Science, 1982; 217 : 267–269.

5. Belizan, J. M., Villar, J. et al – Reduction of blood pressure with calcium supplementation in young adults, JAMA, 1983 : 249 : 1161–1165.

6. Hartroff, W. S. et al – Brit. Med. J., 1 : 423, 1949.

7. Nishizawa, 4. et al – J. Vitaminol, 3 : 106, 1957.

8. Best, C. H. et al – Fed. Proc., 8 : 610, 1949.

9. Saunders, J. B., Beevers, D. G. et al – Alcohol intake and hypertension, Lancet. 2 : 653–656, 1981.

10. Anton Jayasuriya – Clinical Acupuncture, B. Jain Publishers, N. Delhi, 1987.

17. PREVENTION OF HIGH BLOOD PRESSURE

Prevention is not only better than cure but much cheaper too. This is especially true for high blood pressure because it is a life-time disease, once established.

High blood pressure and atherosclerosis do not develop overnight. They progress very gradually. Their seeds are sown right in the childhood. Therefore, their preventive measures, too, should be initiated from the childhood.

Negative thinking and type A behaviour play a key role in the development of high blood pressure, coronary heart disease and cerebral haemorrhage. Therefore, try to correctly mould your child's mind. Children mostly imitate the nature, the behaviour and life style of their parents. If your behaviour and nature are sublime, you will set a fine and safe example for your children.

It has been proven again and again that salt is a mineral poison. Yet we use salt recklessly. We shudder even at the thought of eating a saltless diet. In fact we have ourselves accepted the slavery of salt. And we cultivate its addiction in our children too. Salt caters only to our tongue, not to our health. Those who have not had the opportunity to eat salt in their life, find its taste totally disagreeable. If you wish to keep high blood pressure at bay, curtail the use of salt yourselves and insist that your children do the same.

Convince your children of the value of regular exercise. If you do exercises regularly, your children will not refuse to do exercises. Exercises keep the heart healthy and prevent obesity.

Children imitate their parents' dietary habits. Always keep this in mind and remain on your alert about what you eat and drink. See that your children do not develop an excessive liking for sugar, jaggery, chocolates, peppermints, cakes, jam, jelly, biscuits, butter and ghee. See to it that your children only eat moderately and do not become fat. Remember that fat children are not healthy.

Bad habits like smoking and drinking are mostly passed on to children by their parents. If you wish that your children do not develop such habits, it is imperative that you, too, do not smoke or drink.

If you do not correctly care for your children during their growing years, you shall be responsible for the dreadful diseases they might suffer from later in life.

Chapter in a nutshell :

1. The old adage, 'Prevention is better than cure' is especially true for high blood pressure.

2. The importance of incorrect mental attitude in the development of high blood pressure cannot be overemphasized. Parents should mould their children's minds in such ways that they do not develop a type A behaviour.

3. A person desirous of preventing high blood pressure should develop correct dietary habits, eat only in moderation, cut down the intake of salt and see to it that he does not become overweight.

4. All fathers who wish that their children do not smoke or drink, should themselves give up such vices. It is better to do what one preaches.

INSTRUCTIVE CASE HISTORIES

[With a view to making the reader's understanding of diabetes and high blood pressure, their complexities and the finer points of management as clear as daylight, a few case-histories have been presented here.]

(1)

I am a student of arts at the Jaihind college, Mumbai.

My troubles started when I went on a month-long tour to North India, along with my college-friends. A constant raging thirst started harassing me. I used to empty into my mouth lassi, plain water, aerated waters and all other drinks I could lay my hands on. I also passed a large amount of urine and quite frequently so. In fact I was aroused 3 – 4 times during the night by an intense desire to pass urine. My hunger, too, had become very acute. I ate almost double the food I used to consume previously. However, my digestive powers were not good enough to digest so much food. I used to pass sticky, semi-solid or loose stools. Fatigue and weakness troubled me to such an extent that I prefered staying back in the hotel to going sightseeing. My friends commented time and gain on the paleness of my face. My clothes were gradually becoming loose, making me realise that I was losing weight.

My parents were taken aback by my lean appearance when I returned home. On the same evening, they dragged me to our family doctor, who is a homoeopath. He attributed my trouble to dysentry and prescribed a treatment – course. He also advised me to eat nourishing and fattening food so that I could regain my lost weight. How he missed the correct diagnosis, God only knows.

Well, I started right away in my efforts to regain my old weight. I started consuming dry fruits, sweetened milk, fruit juices, butter, honey and a number of other nutritious foods. It goes without saying that my condition worsened. The quantity of urine increased. A constant, nagging abdominal pain arose. A sweetish odour enriched my breaths. I felt drowsy and slept throughout the day.

One evening my mother persuaded me to go shopping, thinking that the stroll will brighten me up. I felt giddy and collapsed in the market.

When I awoke next morning, I was in a hospital. My mother was sitting beside me. I had a tube in my handvein, through which electrolytes were being introduced into my blood. My mother evaded my querries about my malady. But the doctor who came to examine me was most candid. 'A blood-sample had been drawn from your vein for investigations; you have diabetes,' he said. Tears rushed into my eyes. But I lay still keeping my eyes closed. The doctor wanted to discuss with me the facts about my disease but my mother pleaded with him to leave me alone for the time being.

Nobody in my family had ever suffered from this disease. Then why was I affected? I had been affected by mumps in my childhood. But I never had any other disease. The more I thought, the more I got depressed.

In the afternoon, I fell asleep. When I awoke, my grandmother had come to see me. My mother requested her to look after me for a while and went off for a bath. My grandmother opened her bag to bring out a lunch box. She had brought for me, my favourite dish—dudhi halwa. I finished it off within no time. At around 7 in the evening my abdominal pain returned and my breathing became laboured. My mother rushed to call the doctor. My condition surprised him. 'Did you give Meena anything to eat?' he asked my mother. My mother replied in the negative. He reiterated the question. I finally broke my silence. 'I have had halwa,' I said. The doctor stood there in silence, visibly annoyed. Finally, he enlightened me about my disease, about the prohibited foods, about the symptoms of high blood sugar (hyperglycemia) as well as those of low blood sugar (hypoglycemia). He strictly warned me against eating or drinking anything without his or the nurse's knowledge or consent.

Insulin is inevitable for the treatment of my disease. But it cannot be taken orally because it is digested and rendered ineffective by the digestive juices. Hence it has to be administerred by an injection. I had to take an injection of insulin (40 units) daily. Gradually, I was trained to inject insulin myself. Finally I returned home with a good amount of knowledge about my disease and its management.

Time passed. Apart from the fact that I had to inject insulin into my body and refrain from eating certain foods, I led an almost normal life.

I had the first experience of hypoglycemia (abnormally low blood sugar) 7 months after the onset of my illness. I had taken an insulin injection at around 10.00 a.m. After lunch I was reading a tense and thrilling detective novel. Criminal Gulam Ali, confounded by detective Dinesh Kumar was sweating profusely and trembling with fear. I, too, was sweating and shivering. I was feeling extremely hungry, but I did not have the strength to call my mother. My eyes were open, but I could hardly see. My ears were open but I could not hear. My mind had been blanked. I could do nothing but lie down. At last my mother entered with a cup of tea. My condition terribly frightened her and she ran to call the doctor staying in the nearby building. However, my spirit had soared at the sight of tea. By the time the doctor came, I had drunk the tea and was feeling much better.

The doctor examined me. He wished to examine my medicines. On seeing the insulin bottle he asked me, "Do you require 80 units of insulin daily?' This question made me realise that the drug-store salesman had by oversight given me a 80 unit insulin bottle instead of the usual 40 unit bottle. My blood sugar level had naturally plunged too low, causing the untoward symptoms.

My second experience of hypoglycemia was more dramatic. Our college was celebrating the annual sports day. I was to participate in two sports events. I left my home quite early. My events were scheduled in the morning. I was expecting both the events to get completed in the morning itself so that I would go home and have my lunch. But due to various reasons, those events were delayed. Expecting an announcement any moment, I could not leave the place. I was very hungry but could do nothing about it. Finally my turn came at 2 p. m. The first event was the long jump, in which I fared quite well to be placed third. The second event was the 1500 metre run.

With the sound of the whistle, I started running with all my might. But after running just a short distance, I felt that my strength was fast getting exhausted. I was sweating profusly and shivering. But I kept running to prevent embarrassment. Finally dark clouds loomed large in front of my eyes and I collapsed right on the field. There was a flutter in the audience. A doctor who was present there hurried towards me. I always wear a locket on my neck, on which is written, 'I am a diabetic'. The doctor saw the locket and at once realised the situation. He lost no time to get me to a nearby hospital, where prompt treatment prevented any untoward incident.

A diabetic may have to face hypoglycemia as well as hyperglycemia quite frequently in his life. Their incidence, however, can be minimised with proper care and awareness.

A diabetic should always consume some food before embarking on an unaccustomed or unusual exertion. This will prevent the blood-sugar level from going too low. Similarly with proper care, blood-sugar can be prevented from soaring too high. In short, I have come to realise that for a diabetic, food is a medicine and not a means of pleasure.

Life has become a constant source of wonders for me. While performing the day to day chores, I suddenly realise that I am not just working but living too. I have become less confident in myself. But my confidence in human beings and humanity has increased. People totally unknown to me have come to my assistance when I needed it badly.

In fact the disease gives me new friends every day. I have accepted the challenge posed to me by my disease. This struggle has awakened the poetess in me.

I am no longer ashamed of my disease. Previously I used to hide it from my near and dear ones. But now I openly talk about my disease. Lokmanya Tilak and Swami Vivekanand were diabetics. Stanley Laurel (of the famous Laurel and Hardy duo) was a diabetic. Great writes Ernest Hemmingway and H. G. Wells had diabetes.

I am aware of the fact that I may have to face the long-term complications of diabetes later in my life. But I am not unduly worried. After all, it is the quality of life that matters and not the quantity.

I have only one suggestion for the diabetics. Understand your disease thoroughly. Such knowledge will drive away the fear from your mind and will enable you to lead an active life. An expert's guidance is desirable at every stage of this disease.   — Meena Zaveri, Walkeshwar, Mumbai.

②

Mine is a sedentary occupation. Consequently I am obese. To prevent further weight-gain, I have cultivated the habit of early-morning walks.

One morning, as I was walking bare-footed on dewsoaked grass, my big toe crashed against a sharp stone. A deep wound resulted. When signs of healing did not show up in spite of week-long treatment and dressings, my family doctor urged me to get my urine and blood examined. He gave me a note for the same. Investigations revealed diabetes. My father, too, had diabetes. Thus I had inherited the disease. It was now clear that frequent urination, undue fatigue, lack of concentration, fluctuations in my spectacle numbers and other mild symptoms that I had experienced during the past few days had been caused by diabetes.

I wanted to have a discussion with my doctor about the disease, its complications and its management. But the crowd of patients sitting outside made me realise that he could not give me that much time. He prescribed a medicine (Diabinese–250 mg.) for me and advised me to see him time and again. But I was determined to acquire knowledge. I procured a book on diabetes from the nearby book-shop. I not only learnt about what to eat and what not to eat but also put my knowledge into practice. I also started taking the medicine.

In a short period, my toe-wound healed and all the symptoms of the disease vanished. During the next seven months I frequently suffered from gastric irritation or abdominal pain. But I did not give them much attention.

Thereafter, however, excessive urination, excessive thirst and other symptoms gradually raised their heads again. I chose to wait for a few days hoping that this was a passing phase. But when the troubles showed no respite, I was compelled to see my doctor again. As per his advice, I got my urine and blood examined again. Sugar was present in the urine and the blood-sugar level was considerably above the normal limit. The doctor ascribed this development to a phenomenon termed 'secondary failure' of the medicine. He pointed to the necessity of increasing the dose of the medicine. But this left me thinking. Will the drug-dosage have to be increased time and again? Will not the risk of side-effects increase with the increase in drug-dosage? Are there other harmless and effective measures that can be resorted to for the control of my disease?

This thought-process led me next morning to Dr. Gala. I apprised him of the situation and of my troubles. He wished to obtain a detailed knowledge about my diet and my physical activities. He had to agree that my diet was principally correct. Yet, he cut down the total quantity of food since according to him, losing extra weight was of supreme importance for me. He formulated for me, a whole-day diet plan. He also indicated the need for physical exertion. Contracting muscles, he said, would use up considerable glucose from the blood, thus disburdening the pancreas. I informed him about my morning walk regimen. He requested me to gradually increase the distance and pace of walking. Besides, he also gave me a table of simple yogasanas, which were likely to stimulate my pancreas. I requested him to give me appropriate magnets for starting Magnet therapy at my home and also gained the knowledge about Acupressure points useful in diabetes. 'For a few days, continue with the same dose of the medicine', he said, as I rose to take his leave.

I put all the suggested measures into practice in right earnest. That night, I was not awakened from my sleep by the desire to urinate. Excessive thirst, too, gradually subsided. I had previously read about the Benedict's test to detect the presence (or absence) of sugar in the urine, but had never ventured to perform it. Now, however, its need was imminent. I purchased the necessary equipment and reagents from the market and put my knowledge into action. My urine was free of glucose!

On the fourth day after commencing the various non-medicinal measures, I suffered from bouts of giddiness. My hunger had also increased. I decided to wait and watch. When these symptoms persisted on the following day, I phoned Dr. Gala. He advised me to go for a fresh blood-sugar estimation. The blood-sugar level turned out to be below normal! This, then, was the cause of my symptoms. What now to do about the medicine? I was puzzled. Then coming to a decision, I reduced the drug-dosage from 250 mg. to 200 mg. (2 tablets of 100 mg. strength). For the next five days, things went alright. Of course, I had been examining my urine everyday to ascertain the absence of sugar. On the sixth day, symptoms of giddiness, acute hunger and shivering reappeared. When these symptoms persisted on the following day, I further cut down the drug dosage to 150 mg. Needless to say that I continuously monitored my urine. It contained no sugar. Symptoms of low blood sugar did not arise thereafter.

When I met Dr. Gala again, I informed him of my experiments. He emphatically said that changing the drugdosage on one's own, without a doctor's consent, was incorrect. But I had realised that in the treatment of diabetes, a patient had to shoulder a responsibility even greater than that of a doctor. I had already resolved to be the captain of my treatment-ship. Besides, I had ascertained, through regular urine tests, the fact that I was plying in the right direction.

I have meticulously and zealously followed the above treatment during the past one and a half years. I have succeeded in reducing my weight by 10 kg. My experiments have given me a new and deep insight into my disease and its control. I have come to understand that the treatment of diabetes is an art of maintaining blood-sugar levels within a narrow range; the treatment of diabetes is a constant effort to achieve a subtle balance between the glucose input (throught food) and the glucose utilisation (through medicines, exercise, Magnet Therapy and Acupressure).

Today I am completely aware of my body and of my habits. I take all possible care to prevent a skin–injury or a foot-injury. I may have to face long-term complications of diabetes. How I wish that I had realised the importance of correct dietary habits, regular exercise and preventing obesity much earlier in my life. I may have passed on the seed of this disease to my children. But I am taking all steps to prevent these seeds from germinating, by insisting upon my children to eat the right food and do regular exercise.

It is a deplorable fact that most of our countrymen are careless about their health. They do not consider their well-being as their personal responsibility. They do nothing to prevent a disease. When the disease strikes, they run helter-skelter for medical assistance. A cure, however, is not always possible. Even when achieved, it turns out to be too expensive. It is precisely because of such trends, that serious and incurable diseases like diabetes are on the rise.

— Mansukhlal Shah, C. P. Tank, Mumbai

(3)

My troubles of excessive urination and excessive thirst first started in April–May '86. Before that, I never had to get up during the night to urinate. But now I was awakened 2–3 times during the night by an intense desire to pass urine. I blamed the hot weather for my excessive thirst.

In June, I had to go to Delhi for a 15–day business trip. Irregular routines and rich foods taken with my business associates led to a worsening of my condition. My thirst had become so acute that I gulped whatever drink I came across. By the evening, I used to feel so tired and run down that I preferred lying down on my hotel-bed to furthering my business.

When I returned home, my wife at once commented on my pale face and emaciated condition. All I could do was to hold the long journey responsible.

On the same evening, I had to attend a party, held to celebrate the birthday of my cousin's son. There I met a doctor-friend. When the doctor, after we had exchanged pleasantaries, inquired about my health. I talked to him about my strange complaints. He recommended that my urine and blood be investigated without delay.

These examinations revealed that I had diabetes. I was slightly shocked but not surprised. My father, my uncle and my elder brother all had this disease.

I met my doctor-friend at his consulting room. He consoled me. He indicated that the treatment would include not only medicine, but diet and exercise too. 'I will have to stop eating rice, potatoes and sweets, isn't it, doctor?' I retorted. He smiled. 'That a diabetic just cannot eat rice and potatoes, is a misbelief. Yes, sweets and concentrated sugars should be avoided. But a diabetic's diet is not entirely different from that of others.' He instructed me about what to eat, what not to eat and how to exercise. He also prescribed a medicine (Diabinese) and advised me to see him at regular intervals.

I did start taking his medicine; but on encountering its side-effects like gastric irritation and abdominal pain, I stopped it abruptly. I have great faith in Ayurveda. Hence I visited a wellknown Ayurvedic physician. He advised me to have a glass of karela-juice every morning. Besides he gave me fifteen small packets of a medicine, which he said, was extremely effective in diabetes. ' Your diabetes will have no option but to bid you goodbye very soon.' he said. The confidence and assurance in his voice elevated my spirits.

I started taking his medicine. I kept my diet simple. However, occasionally I did have sweets too. All symptoms of the disease had disappeared and I was feeling very well. Every fifteen days, I sent my servant to the Ayurvedic physician to collect the medicine packets. Two months elapsed.

Thereafter the troubles of urination and thirst gradually reappeared. But I did not pay much attention to the fact. One evening, however, I developed acute abdominal pain, my breathing became laboured and I had bouts of vomitting. Terrified, I rushed to the Ayurvedic physician. But he was out of town. I had no alternative but to go back to my doctor-friend.

He examined me. He said that my condition clearly indicated that sugar had accumulated in my blood, i. e., my diabetes had worsened. He scolded me for not seeing him even once during the past two and a half months. 'But with the Ayurvedic medicine, I was feeling quite well,' I said. Only after my statement did he realise that I was taking a different medicine and not the one prescribed by him.

It was quite evident from his face that he was annoyed. But he kept his cool. The statement he made thereafter is important for all diabetics. He said, **'Absence of external symptoms and an objective feeling of well-being is no proof of the control of the disease. For that purpose, periodical examination of the blood and everyday-examination of the urine. (by the patient himself) are inevitable.** A long delay in the correct treatment may even cause unconsciousness'.

I immediately got my blood examined from a pathological laboratory. The doctor's stand was vindicated when the concentration of sugar in my blood was found to be 395 mg. %.

Thereafter, my blood-sugar was brought down by Diabinese. I am now most particular about my diet. I exercise regularly. I have learnt the art of examining my urine myself. This helps me to ascertain the degree of control (of my disease) achieved.

I have had no complaint during the past 8 months.

— **Laxmidas Sharma, Wadala, Mumbai**

(4)

It happened in June '84.

My right thigh developed a boil. Thinking that it will subside on its own, I did not pay much attention to it. The boil, however, grew larger day after day. Walking had become painful and difficult for me. Even after a week, the large boil showed no signs of bursting open. Finally, on my neighbour's advice, I visited a well-known hakim of Null Bazar area and got an ointment applied to the boil-area.

On removing the dressing two days later, a pus-filled mouth was observed on the boil. A slight pressure opened up the boil and pus surfaced. I bore a lot of pain to evacuate the pus completely. Thereafter I applied a common antiseptic cream on the wound and effected a dressing. But when signs of healing were not seen 4 days later, I got worried and contacted my family doctor. He cleansed the wound and dressed it up. Besides, he also advised me to get my urine examined the next morning.

The finding that my urine possessed 0.5 per cent sugar shocked me. Nobody in my family ever had this disease. I did not talk about the development to my family–members but rushed to the doctor. He consoled me and prescribed me a drug (Rastinon). Usually I stay away from drugs, but this time, the desire for rapid healing of the thigh-wound drove me to the medical store. Thus I started taking the medicine. The next two days (Saturday and Sunday) were holidays and I stayed home, feeling quite well.

I was late to get up on the Monday morning. I had a hurried lunch at 10 a.m. and left for my office. At around 4 p.m. on that day I experienced uneasiness and undue fatigue. I took an early leave and left for my home. I was very hungry. I stood at the bus-stop day-dreaming of a nice snack. The summer sun, the public crowd and the noisy vehicles, were all irritating me. Buses sped past, without stopping. My body had started shivering. A bus stopped at last and I made my way into it. Thereafter for the next few minutes, I was in a sort of a trance, ignorant of my surroundings. I was aroused by the shout of the bus conductor. My stop had come. I hurried to get down. Weakness and shivering had increased. I was sweating profusely. I dragged myself forward wishing to reach home as soon as possible. I could see my building right in front. I only had to cross a road. But right in the middle I felt giddy and collapsed. The scream of the brakes of a motor car which had been forced to stop quite close to me dashed against my ears. A major mishap had been averted. A crowd gathered around me. Fortunately an acquaintance saw me and took me to my residence. Though semi-conscious, I was more than happy to gulp down the tea offered by my wife. Soon I felt better.

The same evening I approached my family doctor again. He advised me to undergo glucose tolerance test, the next morning. The test revealed a surprising fact. Though sugar was escaping in my urine, my blood sugar levels were absolutely normal (fasting 100 mg.%, one hour after the glucose meal 145 mg.% and 2 hours after the glucose meal 105 mg.%). This was a clear indication that my renal threshold for glucose (glucose handling capacity of my kidneys) was abnormally low so that in spite of my blood-sugar values being normal, I was losing sugar in my urine. This is a harmless and benign condition termed 'renal glycosuria'. In short, I did not have diabetes.

I had taken a medicine to decrease the amount of blood sugar in spite of the fact that my blood-sugar level was normal. Consequently, the concentration of glucose in my blood progressively decreased, various body-cells and the brain were deprived of nutrition, untoward symptoms arose and I was saved by the skin of my teeth.

Instead of guessing that I have diabetes since my urine has sugar, if the doctor had advised glucose tolerance test right away, such undesirable circumstance would not have arisen. In fact, glucose tolerance test is inevitable for the diagnosis of diabetes.

It goes without saying, that with adequate care, the wound on my thigh healed.

— **Sitaram Pathak, Worli, Mumbai**

(5)

I run a colour and hardware store in Jabalpur, Madhya Pradesh.

In May '86, I had approached my septagenerian family doctor for the treatment of my cough. As a routine procedure, he examined my blood pressure and found it to be 155/100. I felt a bit nervous and worried when I heard the figures. But the doctor reassured me by saying that if the higher figure (systolic blood pressure) is equal to '100 plus the person's age,' the blood pressure should be considered normal. He said that nothing needed to be done for the blood pressure.

During the next one year, I did suffer from palpitations or mild chest pain occasionally. But I attributed the symptoms to gas and indigestion and carried on as usual.

On the evening of 25th April, I was climbing the staircase of one of my client's building, when I felt a crushing or squeezing pain in my chest, I felt breathless too. Realising that this was not indigestion but something else, I rushed to a heart specialist. He examined me. My blood pressure measured 165/110. The cardiogram, luckily, showed no abnormality. 'Considering that I am 54, my blood pressure cannot be considered high, isn't it doctor?' I asked. 'The blood pressure has no relation to the age and should not be higher than 130/90.' he said. I was surprised. I was reminded of the opinion of my family doctor. 'My blood pressure was 155/100 an year back,' I said. The specialist commented that treatment should have been started at that time and that I had lost an year. He prescribed me a medicine and advised me to see him every fortnight. The medicine brought down my blood pressure to 130/90. Time passed. I was frequently troubled by the drug's side-effects but continued to take it fearing grave consequences if I stopped.

In Nov. 1987, I had to visit Mumbai, as my cousin Rameshchandra's son was getting married. On hearing my story, Rameshchandra took me to Dr. Gala.

Dr. Gala examined me. At that time my blood pressure was 135/95 and weight 79 kg. According to the doctor, this weight was 20 per cent higher than the ideal weight for my height and build. I agreed. I was obese since years because my occupation was sedentary. I loved eating. Every evening we had a fried dish. I smoked too. Finally, I was diagnosed as having a 'type A personality' on the basis of a questionnaire.

The doctor suggested that at the outset, I should reduce my weight. He recommended that I study one of his books, 'From Fat to Fit' for the purpose. Saying that the 'type A' personality almost always leads to high blood pressure, he requested me to bring about a change in my outlook and my behaviour. He suggested a few tricks and drills to achieve this change. He also enlightened me of the ways to reduce mental tension. Heeding to my request, he formulated a 'whole-day diet plan' for me. I saw that the diet restricted the use of salt and fats (ghee, oil, etc.). The doctor also gave me a magnetic belt to be worn on my right wrist and informed me about the Acupressure points useful in high blood pressure. I took his leave saying that all these measures can be implemented only after I return to Jabalpur. He suggested that after I start the treatment, I should gradually decrease the dose of the medicine, under my family doctor's supervision.

After reaching Jabalpur, I commenced Dr. Gala's treatment in right earnest. My efforts were handsomely rewarded. During the next one and a half months, I could gradually cut down the dose of my medicine. Today, my blood pressure remains steady at 130/90 in spite of the fact that I take only half the previous dose of the medicine. I have maintained correspondence with Dr. Gala.

—Kewalchand Mishra, Jabalpur (Madhya Pradesh)

APPENDIX 1 : FOOD SUBSTITUTION

1. CEREALS

Each item tabulated below furnishes nutrition worth 100 calories and any one can be substituted by another.

No.	Item	Quantity or Measure	Weight of the flour or whole	Weight after cooking
1	Chapati (Very thin i. e., Phulka)	2	30 gm. flour	35 gm.
2	Chapati (with some oil)	1	25 gm. flour	35 gm.
3	Jowar bhakhri	$\frac{1}{2}$	30 gm. flour	40 gm.
4	Paratha (with 1 teaspoon oil)	$\frac{1}{2}$	25 gm. flour	40 gm.
5	Bhatura	1	15 gm. flour	30 gm.
6	Puri (with 1 teaspoon oil)	2	15 gm. flour	35 gm.
7	Sliced bread	2 slices	—	40 gm.
8	Khakhra	2	25 gm. flour	30 gm.
9	Cooked rice	1 cup (150 ml)	30 gm. rice	100 gm.
10	Vegetable Pulav (with 1 teaspoon oil)	$\frac{1}{2}$ cup	15 gm. rice	60-70 gm.
11	Khichri	1 cup	30 gm. of rice & pulse	100 gm.
12	Pop Corn	4 table -spoons	—	25 gm.

2. FATS

Each item furnishes nutrition worth 50 calories

No.	Item	Measure	Weight
1	Oil	1 teaspoon	5 gm.
2	Butter, ghee, vanaspati, margarine	1 teaspoon	5 gm.
3	Cream (thick)	1 tablespoon	15 gm.
4	Cream (thin)	2 tablespoons	15 gm.
5	Mayonnaise	1 teaspoon	5 gm.
6	French dressing	3 tablespoons	15 gm.

3. PULSES

Each item furnishes nutrition worth 50 calories and one can be substituted by another.

No.	Item	Measure/ Quantity	Weight after cooking
1	Usal (20 gm. whole mung + $\frac{1}{2}$ teaspoon oil)	$\frac{1}{2}$ cup	80 gm.
2	Usal (20 gm. whole chana + $\frac{1}{2}$ teaspoon oil)	$\frac{1}{2}$ cup	50 gm.
3	Thick dal, Amti (15 gm. dal + some jaggery)	$1\frac{1}{2}$ cup	120 gm.
4	Tur dal or varan (30 gm. dal)	$\frac{3}{4}$ cup	110 gm.
5	Mung dal (20 gm. dal + 1 teaspoon oil)	$\frac{1}{2}$ cup	75 gm.
6	Udad dal (20 gm. dal + $\frac{3}{4}$ teaspoon ghee)	$\frac{1}{2}$ cup	80 gm.
7	Sambhar (25 gm. dal + spices)	1 cup	150 gm.
8	Rasam (with 1 teaspoon oil)	2 cups	230 gm.
9	Chhole (white gram $\frac{2}{3}$ tablespoon)	$\frac{1}{3}$ cup	70 gm.
10	Papad (deep fried)	2	20 gm.
11	Roasted gram	$\frac{1}{2}$ cup	30 gm.
12	Roasted peas	$\frac{1}{2}$ cup	30 gm.

4. FRUITS

Each item tabulated below furnishes nutrition worth 100 calories and one can be substituted by another.

No.	Fruit	Measure/Quantity	Weight
1	Apple	1, big	200 gm.
2	Banana	1, medium	100 gm.
3	Custard apple	1, medium	100 gm.
4	Grapes	24 – 30 nos.	140 gm.
5	Chikoo	1, big	100 gm.
6	Jambu/Jamun	20 nos.	140 gm.
7	Ripe mango	1, medium	200 gm.
8	Orange	1, medium	200 gm.
9	Melon	3 slices	600 gm.
10	Papaya	$\frac{1}{2}$, medium	300 gm.
11	Peaches	3, medium	400 gm.
12	Pear	1, medium	200 gm.
13	Plums	4 – 5, medium	200 gm.
14	Pineapple	3 slices	180 gm.
15	Pomegranate	1, medium	150 gm.
16	Sweet lemon	1, medium	200 gm.
17	Ripe tomatoes	4, medium	500 gm.
18	Water melon	$\frac{1}{4}$, medium	500 gm.

5. DRY FRUITS

Each item tabulated below furnishes nutrition worth 100 calories and one can be had instead of another :

No.	Item	Measure/Quantity	Weight
1	Dried dates	4 – 5 nos.	30 gm.
2	Walnut	3 – 4 nos.	15 gm.
3	Peanuts	25 nos.	15 gm.
4	Roasted peanuts	50 nos.	20 gm.
5	Cashew nuts	6 nos.	17 gm.
6	Almonds	5 nos.	15 gm.
7	Pistachio	10 nos.	16 gm.
8	Dried grapes (Kismis)	5 – 6 nos.	30 gm.

6. MILK

Each item tabulated below supplies nutrition worth 100 calories and any one can be substituted by another :

No.	Item	Measure
1	Buffalo's milk	$\frac{1}{2}$ cup
2	Cow's milk	1 cup
3	Skimmed milk	$1\frac{1}{2}$ cup
4	Curd (made from buffalo's milk)	$\frac{1}{2}$ cup
5	Curd (made from cow's milk)	1 cup
6	Buttermilk (100 gm. curd+required water)	$1\frac{1}{2}$ cup
7	Cheese (made from whole milk)	15 gm.
8	Cheese (made from skimmed milk)	35 gm.
9	Mava (made from buffalo's milk)	35 gm.
10	Mava (made from cow's milk)	35 gm.
11	Condensed milk (sweetened)	5 teaspoons

7. NON-VEGETARIAN FOODS

Each item tabulated below furnished nutrition worth 100 calories and any one can be substituted by another.

No.	Item	Measure/ Quantity	Weight after cooking
1	Ham	1 thin slice	100 gm.
2	Chicken	$\frac{1}{2}$ thin slice	25 gm.
3	Bacon	2 slices	60 gm.
4	Chicken Soup	2 cups	400 – 450 gm.
5	Mutton chops	$2\frac{1}{2}$ slices	25 gm.
6	Sausage	$\frac{1}{2}$ piece	20 gm.
7	Mutton Curry (with 1 teaspoon oil)	1/3 cup	200 gm.
8	Fish Curry (with 1 teaspoon oil)	$\frac{1}{3}$ cup	200 gm.
9	Omelette (1 egg + 2 teaspoons oil)	3/4 piece	50 gm.
10	Deep fried fish	1 piece	40 gm.
11	Deep fried egg	3/4 piece	50 gm.
12	Boiled egg	2	50 gm.
13	Roasted chicken	1 piece	50 gm.

APPENDIX 2 : IDEAL WEIGHT CHARTS FOR ADULT MEN AND WOMEN

IDEAL WEIGHT CHART FOR MEN AGED 25 AND ABOVE

Height		Small frame		Medium frame		Large frame	
		weight in		weight in		weight in	
Cm	Ft-inch	Pounds	Kg	Pounds	Kg	Pounds	Kg
158	5' 2"	111 to 120	50.5 to 54.5	118 to 129	53.5 to 58.5	126 to 141	57 to 64
160	3"	115 to 123	52 to 56	121 to 133	55 to 61	129 to 144	58.5 to 65
163	4"	118 to 126	53.5 to 57	124 to 136	56 to 62	132 to 148	60 to 67
165	5"	121 to 129	55 to 58.5	127 to 139	57.5 to 63	135 to 152	61 to 69
168	6"	124 to 133	56 to 60	130 to 143	58.5 to 65	138 to 156	62.5 to 71
170	7"	128 to 137	58 to 62	134 to 147	60 to 66.5	142 to 161	64.5 to 73
173	8"	132 to 141	60 to 64	138 to 152	62.5 to 69	147 to 166	66.5 to 75
175	9"	136 to 145	62 to 66	142 to 156	64.5 to 71	151 to 169	68.5 to 77
178	10"	140 to 150	63.5 to 68	146 to 160	66 to 72.5	155 to 174	70 to 79
180	11"	144 to 154	65 to 70	150 to 165	68 to 75	159 to 179	72 to 81
183	6' 0"	148 to 158	67 to 71.5	154 to 170	70 to 77	164 to 184	74 to 83.5
185	1"	152 to 162	69 to 73.5	157 to 175	71.5 to 79	168 to 189	76 to 85.5
188	2"	156 to 167	71 to 76	162 to 180	73.5 to 81.5	173 to 194	78.5 to 88
190	3"	160 to 171	72.5 to 77.5	167 to 185	76 to 84	178 to 199	80.5 to 90.5
193	4"	164 to 175	74 to 79	172 to 190	78 to 86	182 to 204	82.5 to 92.5

IDEAL WEIGHT CHART FOR WOMEN AGED 25 AND ABOVE

Height		Small frame weight in		Medium frame weight in		Large frame weight in	
Cm	Ft.-inch	Pounds	Kg	Pounds	Kg	Pounds	Kg
147	4' 10''	92 to 98	42 to 44.5	96 to 107	43.5 to 48.5	104 to 119	47 to 54
150	11''	94 to 101	42.5 to 46	98 to 110	44.5 to 50	106 to 122	48 to 55
152	5' 0''	96 to 104	43.5 to 47	101 to 113	46 to 51	109 to 125	49.5 to 56.5
155	1''	99 to 107	45 to 48.5	104 to 116	47 to 52.5	112 to 128	51 to 58
158	2''	102 to 110	46.5 to 50	107 to 119	48.5 to 54	115 to 131	52 to 59.5
160	3''	105 to 113	47.5 to 51	110 to 122	50 to 55	118 to 134	53.5 to 61
163	4''	108 to 116	49 to 52.5	113 to 126	51 to 57	121 to 138	55 to 62
165	5''	111 to 119	50.5 to 54	116 to 130	52.5 to 58.5	125 to 142	57 to 64.5
168	6''	114 to 123	52 to 56	120 to 135	54.5 to 61	129 to 146	58.5 to 66
170	7''	118 to 127	53.5 to 57.5	124 to 139	56 to 63	133 to 150	60 to 68
173	8''	122 to 131	55 to 59.5	128 to 143	58 to 65	137 to 154	62 to 70
175	9''	126 to 135	57 to 61	132 to 147	60 to 66.5	141 to 158	64 to 71.5
178	10''	130 to 140	58.5 to 63.5	136 to 151	62 to 68.5	145 to 163	66 to 74
180	11''	134 to 144	61 to 65	140 to 155	63.5 to 70	149 to 168	67.5 to 76
183	6' 0''	139 to 148	63 to 67	144 to 159	65 to 72	153 to 173	69.5 to 78.5

APPENDIX 3 : CALORIE COUNTER FOR COMMON UNCOOKED FOODS

Sr. No.	Name of the Food	Moisture in %	Protein in %	Fat in %	Carbohydrate in %	Minerals in %	Fibres in %	Calcium in %	Phosphorous in %	Iron in mg per 100 g	Vitamin 'A' in international units per 100 g	Vitamin 'B' in international units per 100 g	Vitamin 'C' in international units per 100 g	Calories per 100 g
	Cereals													
1	Wheat	12.8	11.8	1.5	71.2	1.5	1.2	0.05	0.32	5.3	108	180	......	348
2	Rice (machine polished)	13.0	6.9	0.4	79.2	0.5	......	0.01	0.11	1.0	0	20	......	348
3	Rice (hand pounded)	12.2	8.5	0.6	78.0	0.7	......	0.01	0.17	2.8	4	60	......	351
4	Barley	12.5	11.5	1.3	69.3	1.5	3.9	0.03	0.23	3.7	......	150	......	335
5	Kaffircorn (Jowar)	11.9	10.4	1.9	74.0	1.8	......	0.03	0.28	6.2	136	115	......	357
6	Rice (flakes) (Pauva)	12.2	6.6	1.2	78.2	1.8	......	0.02	0.22	8.0	......	70	......	350
7	Bajri (Millet)	12.4	11.6	5.0	67.1	2.7	1.2	0.05	0.35	8.8	220	110	......	360
8	Maize (Corn) (Makai)	14.9	11.1	3.6	66.2	1.5	2.7	0.01	0.33	2.1	......	......	......	342
9	Maize Bhutta (Corn) (Makai Bhutta)	79.4	4.3	0.5	15.1	0.7	......	0.01	0.10	0.7	42	......	......	23
10	Samo (Panicum frumentaceum)	11.9	6.2	2.2	65.5	4.4	9.8	0.02	0.28	2.9	trace	......	......	307
	Pulses													
11	Black gram (Udad)	10.9	24.0	1.4	60.3	3.4	......	0.20	0.37	9.8	64	140	......	348
12	Bengal gram (Chana)	9.8	17.1	5.3	61.2	2.7	3.9	0.19	0.24	9.8	316	100	......	316
13	Bengal gram (roasted)	11.2	22.5	5.2	58.9	2.2	......	0.07	0.31	8.9	......	......	......	372
14	Cow pea (Chouli)	12.7	23.4	1.3	59.7	2.9	......	0.08	0.43	4.3	......	......	......	344

15	Red gram (Tuver, tur)	15.2	22.3	1.7	57.2	3.6	.....	0.14	0.26	8.8	220	150	.....	334
16	Green gram (Moong)	10.4	24.0	1.3	56.6	3.6	4.1	0.14	0.28	8.4	158	155	.....	334
17	Lentil (Masur)	12.4	25.1	0.7	59.7	2.1	.....	0.13	0.25	2.0	450	150	.....	346
18	Peas	16.0	19.7	1.1	56.6	2.1	4.5	0.07	0.30	4.4	.....	150	.....	315
19	Field beans (Vaal)	9.6	24.9	0.8	60.1	3.2	1.4	0.06	0.45	2.0	trace	.....	.....	347
20	Soyabean	20.9	43.2	19.5	20.9	4.6	3.7	0.24	0.69	11.5	710	300	.....	432
	Tubers and Edible roots													
21	Colocasia (Alavi)	73.1	3.0	0.1	22.1	.7	.....	0.04	0.14	2.1	40	80	trace	101
22	Ginger	80.9	2.3	0.9	12.3	1.2	2.4	0.02	0.06	2.6	67	.....	6	67
23	Onions	86.8	1.2	0.1	11.6	0.4	.....	0.18	0.05	0.7	.....	40	11	51
24	Carrots	86.0	0.9	0.2	10.7	1.1	1.2	0.08	0.53	1.5	200 to 4300	60	3	47
25	Potatoes	74.7	1.6	0.1	22.9	1.6	.....	0.01	0.03	0.7	40	20	17	99
26	Beetroot	83.8	1.7	0.1	13.6	0.8	.....	0.20	0.06	1.0	trace	70	88	62
27	Radish	94.4	0.7	0.1	4.2	0.4	.....	0.05	0.03	0.04	3	60	15	21
28	Sweet Potatoes (Ratalu)	68.5	1.2	0.3	31.0	1.0	.....	0.02	0.05	0.8	10	.....	24	132
29	Garlic	62.8	6.3	0.1	29.0	1.0	0.8	0.03	0.31	1.3	0	.....	13	142
30	Yam (Suran)	78.7	1.2	0.1	18.4	0.8	.....	0.05	0.02	0.6	434	20	trace	79
	Nuts and Oilseeds													
31	Walnut (Akhrot)	4.5	15.6	64.5	11.0	1.8	2.6	0.10	0.38	4.8	10	150	0	687
32	Linseed (Alasi)	6.6	20.3	37.1	28.8	2.4	4.8	0.17	0.37	2.7	50	.....	0	530
33	Cashew nut (Kaju)	5.9	21.2	46.9	22.3	2.4	1.3	0.05	0.45	5.0	100	.....	0	596
34	Coconut	36.3	4.5	41.6	13.0	1.0	3.6	0.01	0.24	1.7	trace	15	1	444
35	Til	5.1	18.3	43.3	25.2	5.2	2.9	1.45	0.57	10.5	100	.....	0	564
36	Pistachio nut (Pista)	5.6	19.8	53.5	16.2	2.8	2.1	0.14	0.43	13.7	240	.....	0	626

Sr. No.	Name of the Food	Moisture in %	Protein in %	Fat in %	Carbohydrate in %	Minerals in %	Fibres in %	Calcium in %	Phosphorous in %	Iron in mg per 100 g	Vitamin 'A' in international units per 100 g	Vitamin 'B' in international units per 100 g	Vitamin 'C' in international units per 100 g	Calories per 100 g
37	Almond nut (Badam)	5.2	20.8	58.9	10.5	2.0	1.7	0.23	0.49	3.5	trace	80	0	655
38	Ground nut (Peanut) (Moongfali)	7.9	26.7	40.1	20.3	1.9	3.1	0.05	0.39	1.6	63	300	0	549
39	Mustard seeds (Rai)	8.5	22.0	39.7	23.8	4.2	1.8	0.49	0.70	17.9	270	......	trace	541
	Fruits													
40	Pineapple (Ananas)	86.5	7.6	0.1	12.0	0.5	0.3	0.02	0.01	0.9	60	......	63	50
41	Indian gooseberry (Amala)	81.2	0.5	0.1	14.1	0.7	3.4	0.05	0.02	1.2	......	......	600	59
42	Fig (Anjeer)	80.8	1.3	0.2	17.1	0.6	5.6	0.06	0.03	1.2	270	......	2	75
43	Tamarind (ripe) (Amli)	20.9	3.1	0.1	67.4	2.9		0.17	0.11	10.9	100	......	13	283
44	Water-melon (Kalinger)	95.7	0.1	0.2	3.8	0.2		0.11	0.01	0.2	trace	......	1	17
45	Raisins (dry) (Kismis)	18.5	2.0	0.2	77.3	2.0		0.10	0.08	4.0	0	75	trace	319
46	Mangoes (raw)	90.0	0.7	0.1	7.6	0.4	1.1	0.01	0.03	1.7	trace	......	1	39
47	Mangoes (ripe)	86.1	0.6	0.1	8.8	0.3		0.01	0.02	4.5	4800	......	......	50
48	Bananas	61.4	1.3	0.2	36.4	0.7	5.2	0.01	0.05	0.4	trace	50	1	153
49	Wood apple	69.5	7.3	0.6	15.5	1.9	2.1	0.13	0.11	0.6	......	......	......	97
50	Dates (Khajoor)	26.1	3.0	0.2	67.3	1.3		0.07	0.08	10.6	600	30	trace	283
51	Pompelmoose	92.0	0.7	0.1	7.1	0.2		0.02	0.02	0.2	......	40	31	32
52	Guava (Amrood)	76.1	1.5	0.2	14.5	0.8	6.9	0.01	0.04	1.0	trace	......	299	66

53	Rose apple (Jambu)	78.2	0.7	0.1	19.7	0.4	0.9	0.02	0.01	1.0	......	......	......	83
54	Tomatoes (ripe)	94.5	1.0	0.1	3.9	0.5	......	0.01	0.02	0.1	320	40	32	20
55	Pomegranates (Anar)	78.00	1.6	0.1	14.6	0.7	5.1	0.01	0.07	0.3	0	......	16	65
56	Grapes	85.5	0.8	0.1	10.2	0.4	3.0	3.03	0.02	0.4	15	trace	3	45
57	Pears	86.9	0.2	0.1	11.5	0.3	1.0	0.01	0.01	0.7	14	......	trace	47
58	Papaya	89.6	0.5	0.1	9.5	0.4	......	0.01	0.01	0.4	2020	......	46	40
59	Peach	90.1	1.5	0.2	8.9	0.6	......	0.02	0.02	1.5	230	40	1	38
60	Jack-fruit (Fanas)	77.2	1.9	0.2	17.4	0.8	1.1	0.17	0.11	10.9	100	......	03	65
61	Jujube fruit (Bor)	85.9	0.8	0.1	12.8	0.4	......	0.03	0.03	0.8	70	......	......	55
62	Mosambi	84.6	1.5	1.0	10.9	0.7	1.3	0.09	0.02	0.3	26	......	63	59
63	Raspberry	82.7	1.8	0.2	11.5	0.6	3.2	0.01	0.06	1.8	......	......	49	55
64	Lemon	85.0	1.0	0.9	11.1	0.3	1.7	0.07	0.01	2.3	trace	......	39	57
65	Apple	85.9	0.3	0.1	13.4	0.3	......	0.01	0.02	1.7	trace	40	2	56
66	Orange	87.8	0.9	0.3	10.6	0.4	......	0.05	0.02	0.01	350	40	68	49
	Vegetables													
67	Cucumber	96.4	0.4	0.1	2.8	0.3	......	0.01	0.03	1.5	trace	90	7	14
68	Bitter gourd (Karela)	92.4	1.6	0.2	4.2	0.8	0.8	0.02	0.07	2.2	210	24	88	25
69	Plantains (raw-bananas)	83.2	1.4	0.2	14.7	0.5	......	0.01	0.03	0.6	50	15	24	66
70	Plantain flowers	90.2	1.5	0.2	5.0	1.2	1.9	0.03	0.05	0.1	......	......	......	28
71	Cabbage	90.2	1.8	0.1	6.3	0.6	1.0	0.03	0.05	0.8	2000	150	124	30
72	Cauliflower	89.4	3.5	0.4	5.3	1.4	......	0.03	0.06	1.3	38	110	36	39
73	Pumpkin (gourd)	92.6	1.4	0.1	5.3	0.6	......	0.01	0.03	0.7	84	200	2	28
74	Cluster beans	82.5	3.7	0.2	9.9	1.4	2.3	0.13	0.05	5.8	330	......	48	56
75	Chola pods	92.5	0.9	0.1	3.5	1.8	1.2	0.26	0.03	1.8	......	......	......	18
76	Tomatoes (raw)	92.8	1.9	0.1	4.5	0.7	......	0.02	0.04	2.4	320	23	31	27

Sr. No.	Name of the Food	Moisture in %	Protein in %	Fat in %	Carbohydrate in %	Minerals in %	Fibres in %	Calcium in %	Phosphorous in %	Iron in mg per 100 g	Vitamin 'A' in international units per 100 g	Vitamin 'B' in international units per 100 g	Vitamin 'C' in international units per 100 g	Calories per 100 g
77	Tomatoes (ripe)	94.5	1.0	0.1	3.9	0.5	....	0.01	0.02	0.1	320	40	33	20
78	Tindora	92.3	1.7	0.1	5.2	0.6	....	0.02	0.03	0.9	28	......	......	27
79	Ridge gourd	95.4	0.5	0.1	3.7	0.3	....	0.04	0.04	1.6	56	22	......	18
80	Bottle gourd	96.3	0.2	0.1	2.9	0.5	....	0.02	0.01	0.7	trace	......	......	13
81	Parval (long)	94.1	0.5	0.3	4.4	0.7	....	0.05	0.03	1.3	160	......	trace	22
82	Parval (ordinary)	92.3	2.0	0.3	1.9	0.5	3.0	0.03	0.04	1.7	......	......	trace	18
83	Broad beans (Papadi)	82.4	4.5	0.1	10.0	1.0	2.0	0.05	0.06	1.6	221	144	12	59
84	French beans	82.0	1.7	0.1	4.5	1.0	1.8	0.05	0.03	1.7	58	21	14	30
85	Lady's finger	88.0	2.2	0.2	7.7	0.7	1.2	0.09	0.08	1.5	5	15	16	41
86	Brinjals	91.5	1.3	0.3	6.4	0.5	....	0.02	0.06	1.3	139	120	23	34
87	Peas	72.1	7.2	0.1	19.8	0.8	....	0.03	0.08	1.5	trace	40	9	109
88	Turnip (Salgam)	91.1	0.5	0.2	7.6	0.6	....	0.03	0.04	0.4	trace	......	43	34
89	Drumsticks	86.9	2.5	0.1	4.3	2.0	4.8	0.01	0.03	0.6	"	......	18	20
	Leafy Vegetables													
90	Bishop's weed (Ajawan leaves)	81.3	6.0	0.6	8.6	2.1	1.4	0.23	0.14	6.3	5800 to 7500	trace	62	64
91	Alavi leaves	89.4	0.3	0.3	4.2	1.2	0.6	0.06	0.02	0.5	......	......	......	20
92	Carrot leaves	83.3	5.1	0.5	8.3	2.8	....	0.34	0.11	8.8	......	......	......	58
93	Gram leaves	77.8	7.0	1.4	11.7	2.1	....	0.34	0.12	23.8	......	......	......	90
94	Tanka leaves	87.9	4.7	0.4	3.7	3.3	....	0.15	0.08	4.2	......	......	......	37
95	Onion leaves	87.6	0.9	0.2	8.9	0.8	1.6	0.05	0.05	7.5	......	......	......	41

#	Item													
96	Hermaphrodite leaves (Tandaljo leaves)	85.0	3.0	0.3	8.1	3.6	.....	0.08	0.05	22.9	.....	.....	.....	47
97	Hermaphrodite (amaranth) (Tandaljo Leaves) (red)	85.8	4.9	0.5	5.7	3.1	.....	0.50	0.10	21.4	2500 to 11000	173	173	47
98	Coriander leaves	87.9	3.3	0.6	6.5	1.7	.....	0.14	0.06	10.0	10460 to 12600	.....	135	45
99	Betel leaves	85.4	3.1	0.8	6.1	2.5	2.3	0.23	0.04	5.7	9500	.....	5	44
100	Spinach leaves (Palakh leaves)	91.7	1.9	0.9	4.0	1.5	.....	0.06	0.01	5.0	2600 to 3500	70	48	32
101	Mint leaves	83.0	4.8	0.6	8.0	1.6	2.0	0.20	0.08	15.6	2700	.....	.....	57
102	Fenugreek leaves (Methi leaves)	81.8	4.9	0.9	9.8	1.6	1.0	0.47	0.05	16.9	3900	70	.....	67
103	Mustard seeds leaves	84.9	5.1	0.4	7.1	2.5	.....	0.37	0.11	12.5	.....	.....	.....	55
104	Nimb leaves (tender)	59.4	11.6	3.0	21.2	2.6	2.2	0.13	0.19	25.3	4600	.....	.....	158
105	Lettuce	92.9	2.1	0.3	3.0	1.2	0.5	0.05	0.03	2.4	2200	90	15	23
106	Drumstick tree leaves	75.0	6.7	1.7	13.4	2.3	0.9	0.44	0.07	7.0	11300	70	220	94
	Spices and Condiments													
107	Ajawan	8.9	15.4	18.1	38.6	7.1	11.9	1.42	0.30	14.6	.....	.....	.....	379
108	Cardamom (Elaichi)	20.0	10.2	2.2	42.1	5.4	20.1	0.13	0.16	5.0	.....	.....	0	229
109	Nutmeg (Jaiphal)	14.3	7.5	36.4	28.5	1.7	11.6	0.12	0.24	4.6	trace	.....	0	472
110	Mace (Jawantri)	15.9	6.5	24.4	47.8	1.6	3.8	0.18	0.10	12.6	.....	.....	0	437
111	Cumin seeds (Jeera)	11.9	18.7	15.0	36.6	5.8	12.0	1.08	0.49	31.0	870	.....	3	356
112	Coriander seeds	11.2	14.1	16.1	21.6	4.4	32.6	0.63	0.37	17.9	1570	.....	trace	288
113	Chillies	10.0	15.9	6.2	31.6	6.1	30.2	0.16	0.37	2.3	576	.....	50	246
114	Chillies (green)	82.6	2.9	0.6	6.1	1.0	6.8	0.03	0.08	1.2	454	.....	111	41

Sr. No.	Name of the Food	Moisture in %	Protein in %	Fat in %	Carbohydrate in %	Minerals in %	Fibres in %	Calcium in %	Phosphorous in %	Iron in mg per 100 g	Vitamin 'A' in international units per 100 g	Vitamin 'B' in international units per 100 g	Vitamin 'C' in international units per 100 g	Calories per 100 g
115	Pepper (black)	12.9	11.5	6.8	49.5	4.4	14.9	0.46	0.20	16.8	......	......	......	305
116	Fenugreek seeds (Methi)	13.7	26.2	5.8	44.1	3.0	7.2	0.16	0.37	14.1	160	......	0	333
117	Mustard seeds (Rai)	8.5	22.0	39.7	23.8	4.2	1.8	0.49	0.70	17.9	270	......	trace	541
118	Cloves	23.3	5.2	8.9	47.9	5.2	9.5	0.74	0.10	4.9	......	......	0	293
119	Turmeric	13.1	6.3	5.1	69.4	3.5	2.6	0.15	0.28	18.6	50	......	0	349
120	Asafoetida	16.0	4.0	1.1	67.8	7.0	4.1	0.69	0.05	22.2	......	......	0	297
	Milk and Milk preparations													
121	Milk (cow's)	87.6	3.3	3.6	4.8	0.7	......	0.12	0.09	0.2	180	17	2	65
122	Milk (Buffalo's)	81.0	4.3	8.8	5.1	0.8	......	0.21	0.13	0.2	162	......	......	117
123	Milk (Goat's)	85.2	3.7	5.6	4.7	0.8	......	0.17	0.12	0.3	182	......	2	84
124	Milk (Human)	88.0	1.0	3.9	7.0	0.1	......	0.02	0.01	0.2	208	......	2	67
125	Milk (Human) (b.s.) *	92.1	2.5	1.0	4.6	0.7	......	0.12	0.09	0.2	......	......	1	29
126	Milk powder (b.s.) *	......	38.0	0.1	51.0	......	......							357
127	Curd (made from cow's milk)	90.3	2.9	2.9	3.3	0.6	......	0.12	0.09	0.3	130	......	......	51
128	Buttermilk	97.5	0.8	1.1	0.5	0.1	......	0.03	0.03	0.8	trace	......	......	15

* Butter separated

Sr. No.	Name of the Food	Moisture in %	Protein in %	Fat in %	Carbohydrate in %	Minerals in %	Fibres in %	Calcium in %	Phosphorous in %	Iron in mg per 100 g	Vitamin 'A' in international units per 100 g	Vitamin 'B' in international units per 100 g	Vitamin 'C' in international units per 100 g	Calories per 100 g
129	Paneer	40.3	24.1	25.1	6.3	4.2	......	0.79	0.52	0.1	273	......	......	348
130	Khoya (made from buffalo's milk)	30.6	14.6	31.2	20.5	3.1	......	0.65	0.42	5.8	......	–	0	421
131	Khoya (made from buffalo's milk) (b.s.)*	46.1	22.3	1.6	25.7	4.3	......	0.99	0.65	2.7	......	......	0	206
	Non-veg. foods													–
132	Egg (Duck's)	71.0	13.5	13.7	0.7	1.0	......	0.07	0.26	3.0	1200	......	......	180
133	Egg (Hen's)	73.7	13.3	13.3	......	1.0	......	0.06	0.22	2.1	1200	......	......	173
134	Liver (Sheep's)	70.4	19.3	7.5	1.4	1.5	......	0.01	0.38	6.3	22300	120	20	150
135	Honey	......	0.4	......	71.3	......	......	......	......	......	trace	trace	trace	437
136	Fish (small)	77.5	21.5	1.6	......	2.0	......	0.06	0.41	2.3	26	60	......	100
137	Fish (big)	78.4	22.6	0.6	......	0.8	......	0.02	0.19	0.9	......	......	......	91
138	Shrimp (zinga)	77.9	20.8	0.3	......	1.4	......	0.09	0.24	0.8	trace	30	......	86
139	Meat (prawns)	83.5	8.9	1.1	3.4	3.2	......	1.37	0.15	21.2	1300	......	......	59
140	Beef	74.3	22.6	2.6	......	1.0	......	0.01	0.19	0.8	trace	50	2	114
141	Mutton	71.5	18.5	13.3	......	1.3	......	0.15	0.15	2.5	31	60	......	194
142	Pork	77.4	18.7	4.4	......	1.0	......	0.03	0.20	2.3	trace	180	2	114

* Butter separated

APPENDIX 4 : CALORIE COUNTER FOR COOKED OR PROCESSED COMMON FOODS

Sr. No.	Food Item	Approx. Quantity.	Calorie
1	Chapati (Millet) (small)	45 g	108
2	Chapati (Jowar) (small)	45 g	106
3	Chapati (Wheat) (thin)	20 g	40
4	Poori (Wheat)	16 g	68
5	Khakhara (Wheat)	20 g	40
6	Paratha (Wheat)	55 g	304
7	Bread (two slices)	45 g	120
8	Wheat biscuits (two)	20 g	64
9	Khichri/Rice	140 g	238
10	Dal (Watery) (one small bowl)	200 g	105
11	Jam (one spoon)	20 g	58
12	Jelly (one spoon)	20 g	52
13	Squash (Orange/Lemon)	one glass	69
14	Squash (Mango)	one glass	72
15	Butter (one spoon)	5 g	36
16	Cream (one spoon)	15 g	50
17	Ghee (one spoon)	5 g	45
18	Groundnut oil (one spoon)	15 g	126
19	Paneer (one spoon)	30 g	112
20	Ice cream	100 g	196
21	Horlicks, Bournvita, etc. (two spoons)		110
22	Cake (without icing) (one piece)	75 g	218
23	Cake (with icing) (one piece)	90 g	302
24	Pie	160 g	377
25	Pudding (1/2 cup)	105 g	185
26	Idli (1 piece)	68 g	65
27	Upama (One plate)	260 g	397
28	Sada Dosa (one)	100 g	216
29	Masala Dosa	100 g	210
30	Potato Bhajia (four)	60 g	240
31	Onion Bhajia (six)	60 g	197
32	Potato chips (ten)	20 g	108
33	Pattis (one)	60 g	201
34	Potato wada (one)	45 g	118
35	Dahi wada (one)	45 g	83
36	Kachori (one)	45 g	190
37	Cutlets (one)	60 g	126
38	Potato Pauva (1 plate)	60 g	123
39	Sago Khichri (one plate)	45 g	182
40	Samosa (one)	30 g	103
41	Chakari (one)	30 g	170
42	Mesur (one piece)	56 g	345
43	Boondi Laddu (one)	35 g	150
44	Carrot Halwa	85 g	333
45	Dudhi Halwa	85 g	300
46	Glucose (one spoon)	75 g	218
47	Honey (one spoon)	21 g	66
48	Jaggery (one spoon)	15 g	56
49	Sugar (one spoon)	6 g	25
	Non-veg. food items		
50	Egg gravy (one cup)	150 g	181
51	Omelet (one)	40 g	77
52	Fried fish	100 g	245
53	Fried meat	140 g	340
54	Soup (chicken, mutton)	200 g	35
	Beverages		
55	Tea (one cup)	150 g	60
56	Coffee (one cup)	150 g	75
57	Lime juice (one glass)	200 g	75
58	Aerated Drinks (Thums up. Gold Spot, etc.) (one bottle)	200 g	80
59	Beer (one glass)	200 g	100
60	Alcohol (one peg)	45 g	110

APPENDIX 5 : VITAMINS, THEIR FUNCTIONS AND SOURCES

Vitamin	Daily requirement of an adult person	Function	Sources	Symptoms of deficiency
Vitamin 'A'	4000 to 5000 international units	This Vitamin is essential for the preservation and growth of certain cells in the body. It is also essential for preserving health of the eyesight. Our night-vision depends on this vitamin. Besides, it is also essential for the general development of bones and formation of teeth.	Milk, paneer, leafy vegetables, cabbage, carrots, red and yellow vegetables and fruits. Besides, it is also available in large quantities from the liver oil of certain fishes (e.g., cod-liver oil).	Lack of Vitamin 'A' causes slackening of the growth of body. Eyes and skin become dry; night vision is impaired; abnormalities of bone and teeth also develop.
Vitamin 'B' : This is a group of Vitamins comprising eight Vitamins (Vitamins) B₁, B₂, B₆, B₁₂ Niacin, Pantothenic acid, Biotin and Folecin)	Each approximatley 0.5 to 5 mg	Vitamins of this group are essential for the growth of the body, for causing appetite and for the health of eyesight, nervous system and skin. They are also essential for preventing anaemia.	Milk, yeast, wheat bran, sprouted wheat, greenleaf vegetables, cereals, etc. eggs, meat (particularly liver) and fish are also sources of vitamin 'B'.	Lack of vitamin 'B' causes a disease named Beriberi. Lack of vitamin 'B' causes cracks in the skin and around eyes, nose and mouth. Lack of Niacin causes a disease called Pelagra and abnormalities of the nervous system. Lack of Vitamin B causes anaemia and skin diseases. Lack of Pantothenic acid causes metabolic disorders. Symptoms of Biotin and Folecin are similar to those of the lack of Pantothenic acid. Lack of Vitamin B₁₂ causes slackening of the growth of the body and also causes fatal anaemia.

Vitamin	Daily requirement of an adult person	Function	Sources	Symptoms of deficiency
Vitamin 'C'	45 mg	This vitamin is essential for the growth of body. It also makes a vital contribution to the formation of teeth and bones. It helps in keeping the different cells connected to one another. It expedites the process of healing wounds. It enhances the resistance power of the body. It is also associated with the production of Steroid hormones in the body.	Sweet and sour (citrous) fruits, Indian gooseberry (amla), tomatoes, watermelon, guava, cabbage, pineapples, potatoes and green-leaf vegetables are some of the sources of vitamin 'C'.	Besides causing a disease called scurvy, lack of this vitamin may cause problems of teeth and gums, internal haemorrhage, osteoporosis or bones, weight loss and infertility.
Vitamin 'D'	300 to 400 international units	This vitamin is essential for the growth of body. It also makes a vital contribution to the formation of teeth and bones.	Sunlight is the best source of vitamin 'D'. Besides that, it is also available from milk, eggs, and some fish-liver oils.	Deficiency of Vitamin 'D' causes osteoporosis of bones and consequently children develop a disease called Rickets.
Vitamin 'E'	12 to 15 international units	This is an essential vitamin for fertility. Besides that, it also strengthens red blood cells and prevents their disintegration.	Milk, sprouted wheat, green leaf vegetables, vegetable oils, dry fruits (nuts) and eggs.	Deficiency of this vitamin may cause infertility.
Vitamin 'K'	1 to 2 mg	It is essential for producing Prothombin– a substance that is necessary for coagulation of blood.	Wheat, bran, green leaf vegetables, tomatoes, Cauliflower, Soyabean oil, Vegetable oils and animal livers.	Lack of this vitamin hampers the production of Prothombin and consequently blood coagulation does not take place, as a result of which, there is profuse bleeding even after a minor injury.

APPENDIX 6 : MINERALS, THEIR FUNCTIONS AND SOURCES

Mineral	Daily requirement of an adult person	Functions	Sources	Symptoms of Deficiency
Calcium	800 mg	About 99% calcium is in the teeth and bones. It is also essential for free movement of different substances in the cells of body.	Milk and milk preparations, fenugreek, drumstick and similar, other leafy vegetables, beetroot, figs, grapes, water-melon, bajri (millet), til, black gram (udad). Besides these, calcium is available from some types of fish and oyster also.	Lack of calcium causes weakening of bones & teeth and also causes osteoporosis.
Phosphorus	800 mg	About 80% phosphorus is contained in the bones and teeth. It is a vital component of every cell in the body. It helps in maintaining blood pH. Besides, it is also essential for producing vital substances like DNA, RNA and ATP.	Milk, paneer, yeast, dry fruits (nuts), soyabean, dates, carrots, guava, etc. Besides these, it is also available from eggs, fish and meat.	Phosphorus deficiency causes weakening of bones and weightloss.
Potassium	2500 mg	Potassium is an important component of the intracellular fluid. It is essential for the metabolism of carbohydrates and proteins. It also helps in maintaing blood pH.	Fresh fruits, milk, garlic, radish, potatoes and meat contain potassium in large quantities.	Potassium deficiency may cause weakening of muscles, brittleness of bones, infertility and cardiac trouble.

Mineral	Daily requirement of an adult person	Functions	Sources	Symptoms of Deficiency
Sodium	2500 mg	Sodium is an important component of the extracellular fluid. About 30 to 40% sodium is contained in the bones.	Salt, milk, beetroot, carrots, radish, frenchbeans, etc. contain sodium. Besides them, it is also found in eggs, meat and fish.	Sodium deficiency causes headache, nausea, slow growth of body and muscular weakness.
Iron	10 mg	About 70% iron is contained in the haemoglobin. The remaining 26% is contained in the liver, spleen and bones. In absence of iron, cells of the body cannot exchange oxygen.	Fenugreek, mint and similar other green-leaf vegetables, til, bajri (millet) gram, green gram, black gram, soyabean, dates, mangoes, etc. Besides these, it is also obtained from eggs, meat, animal livers, oysters, etc.	Anaemia is the main symptom of iron deficiency.
Sulphur	300 mg	Sulphur is a component of proteins and some vitamins. It is essential for metabolic process in the body.	Beetroot, cabbage, garlic, onions, milk and non-veg. food are some of the chief sources of sulphur.	Sulphur deficiency causes metabolic disorders in the body.
Magnesium	350 mg	About 50% magnesium is contained in the bones. The remaining 50% is contained in the cells. It activates many enzymes in the body and that is why many processes of the body depend on it.	Milk, grains, green vegetables, dry fruits (nuts) and meat contain magnesium.	Magnesium deficiency causes weakening of bones, teeth and muscles. Lack of magnesium may also create cardiac problems.

Mineral	Daily requirement of an adult person	Functions	Sources	Symptoms of Deficiency
Chlorine	2000 mg	This substance works in collaboration with sodium. It is an important component of extracellular fluid. It also activates many enzymes in the body. It is an important component of gastric juices responsible for the digestion of food.	Salt, milk, carrots, apricot, beetroots, frenchbeans, potatoes, spinach, cabbage, tomatoes, bananas, dates, etc. contain chlorine. Besides them, it is also obtained from eggs, meat and sea-fish.	Chlorine deficiency weakens the bones and makes the joints stiff.
Iodine	0.14 mg	It is a component of thyroid gland secretion.	It can be obtained from seafood and green-leaf vegetables.	Iodine deficiency causes thyroid gland disorders and a disease named Goitre.

AUTO-URINE THERAPY

If we can drink the urine of cows, why can't we drink our own urine?

Free your mind of the misguided disgust about urine and regain your lost health.

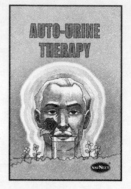

- Has your illness resisted all kinds of treatment?
- Are there no specific medicines for your illness?
- Are you apprehensive about the side-effects of drugs?
- Have you despaired of life?

DO NOT LOSE HOPE.

HAVE RECOURSE TO AUTO-URINE THERAPY.

Our ancient Vedic works too, have recommended the drinking of one's own urine. In the Damar Tantra, composed by Lord Shiva Himself, auto-urine has been described as 'Shivambu', 'Shiva' means 'salubrious or beneficial, and 'ambu' means 'water'. Thus the combined term, 'shivambu' means salubrious water.

- A large number of supposedly incurable diseases have been successfully treated with self-urine. Cases of complete cure of even a disease like cancer have been recorded.
- The idea that urine is nothing but a poisonous waste rejected by the body is a total misconception.
- Barring exceptional cases, fresh urine is always completely free from micro-organisms (bacteria) of all kinds.
- Urine contains hormones, enzymes, vitamins and numerous other nutritive and curative substances.

A book containing a complete exposition of the scientific basis of AUTO-URINE THERAPY.

E 8

Printed by : Chirag Offset Pvt. Ltd., Ahmedab;